Anne's glory box

COLLECTION

Editorial
Managing Editor: Judy Poulos
Editorial Assistant: Ella Martin
Editorial Coordinator: Margaret Kelly

Photography
Andrew Elton

Styling
Lisa Hilton

Illustrations
Lesley Griffith

Design and Production
Managers: Sheridan Carter, Anna Maguire
Picture Editor: Kirsten Holmes
Design: Jenny Pace
Layout: Lulu Dougherty

This edition first published in 1995 by
J.B. Fairfax Press Pty Limited
80-82 McLachlan Ave, Rushcutters Bay,
NSW 2011, Australia
A.C.N. 003 738 430
Formatted by J.B. Fairfax Press Pty Limited
Printed by Toppan Printing Company,
Hong Kong

The contents of this book have been published
previously by J.B. Fairfax Press Pty Limited as
part of the 'Anne's Glory Box' series.

JBFP 413

ANNE'S GLORY BOX COLLECTION
ISBN 1 86343 238 8

Anne's glory box
COLLECTION

Compiled by Gloria McKinnon

J B F P

CONTENTS

WOOL EMBROIDERY 8

Cream-on-Cream Blanket 10

Floral Garden Blanket 12

Rose Blanket 14

In an English Country Garden 16

Bassinet Blanket 18

Garden Lambs Blanket 20

Spring Blossoms 22

Wool-embroidered Shawl 26

HEIRLOOM SEWING 30

Church Dollies 32

Nightgown 34

Peignoir 39

Angel Bunnies 44

Chatelaine 48

Christening Gown Pillowcase *52*

Angel *55*

FOLK ART AND PAPER TOLE *58*

Painted Birdhouse *60*

Paper Tole Nursery *64*

Painted Lamp *67*

Paper Tole Picture *70*

SILK RIBBON EMBROIDERY *74*

Flower Basket Picture *76*

Embroidered Pillows *78*

Embroidered Brooch *80*

Yesterday and Today *82*

Pansy Pillow *85*

Monogrammed Pillow *88*

Embroidered Wallhanging *90*

FLOWER CRAFTS *92*

Floral Foursome *94*

Romantic Swag 96

Christmas Wreath 98

Rose Basket 100

Silk-lined Basket 102

SEWING AND EMBROIDERY 104

Draught Stopper 106

Doll's Dress 109

Velvet-covered Coathanger 112

Shoe Stuffers 115

Crazy Quilt 116

Crazy Quilt Purse 118

Embroidered Pillow 121

Teddy Bear 125

DECOUPAGE 128

Découpage Box 130

Découpage Screen 134

Postcard Box 138

Découpage Brooches *140*

QUILTING *142*

Seven Sisters Quilt *144*

Twilight Garden Quilt *148*

Baby's Spring Garden *151*

Postcards from the Past *154*

Hearts and Hands *158*

Floral Flavours Quilt *163*

Double Wedding Ring Quilt *166*

Baby's Silk Quilt *170*

RIBBON ROSES *174*

Cabbage Rose Cushion *176*

Rose Shoes and Purse *178*

Lace Roses *182*

STITCH GUIDE *184*

INDEX *191*

WOOL EMBROIDERY

Wool embroidery is the perfect choice for the less-than-patient embroiderer. It provides all the beauty of hand-work and has the advantage of 'growing' so quickly that you can see the results develop almost immediately. The effects obtained can be delicate or extravagant, but not at all painstaking.

Traditionally, embroidery with wool has been worked on woollen blanket fabric to produce delicate covers for babies' bassinets and cots. For these pieces, pastel wools are generally worked on pastel backgrounds, as for the Floral Garden Blanket on page 12 or the Garden Lambs Blanket on page 20.

Still working within the boundaries of traditional colour schemes, unusual effects are certainly possible. The Cream-on-Cream blanket on page 10 and the Rose Blanket on page 14 are examples of new directions in this lovely style of embroidery.

Wool embroidery, however, is not restricted to pastel blankets. On page 22, you will find a delightful wool embroidery framed as a picture and, on page 26, a dramatic woollen shawl, lavishly embroidered with flowers.

Cream-on-Cream Blanket

STITCHED BY MARG MANNING

What an exquisite piece this is. Rather than the embroidery contrasting with the wool fabric, this blanket features the delicate effect of cream on cream, accentuated by cream lace and ribbons. You might like to experiment with monochromatic schemes of your own.

Materials

❧ 80 cm x 115 cm/32 in x 45 in cream blanket wool
❧ 8 m/9 yd of 8 cm/3¼ in wide cream edging lace
❧ 4 m/4½ yd of beading
❧ 6 m/6⅔ yd of 7 mm/⁵⁄₁₆ in wide cream silk ribbon
❧ 80 cm/32 in of Vyella for the backing
❧ a variety of wools and threads for the embroidery
❧ matching sewing thread
❧ suitable embroidery and sewing needles
❧ tracing paper and pencil (optional)
❧ bodkin

Method

See the Embroidery Design on Pull Out Pattern Sheet 1.

1 Fold the blanket in half lengthwise and widthwise to find the centre. Mark this point.

2 Baste the outline of the heart on to the blanket, centring it over the middle point. You may wish to trace the outline before you baste it to ensure the heart has a good shape.

3 Embroider the flowers around the heart, using the stitches indicated on the embroidery design. However, don't feel bound by these stitches – use them as a guide only. You may like to experiment with the different threads and wools to decide which one best suits which flower.

4 Join the ends of the edging lace to form a circle. Gather up the straight edge of the lace to fit around the embroidered wool fabric. Pin the lace around the embroidered wool fabric with the straight edge of the lace along the edge of the wool. Adjust the gathers and stitch the lace into place, either by hand or by machine.

5 Place the embroidered wool fabric and the Vyella together with the right sides facing, the raw edges even and the lace sandwiched in between. Stitch around the outside edge with a 1 cm/½ in seam allowance, leaving a 15 cm/6 in opening in one side. Take care not to catch the lace in the stitching. Turn the blanket through to the right side. Slipstitch the opening closed.

6 Handsew the beading around the edge of the front of the blanket. Cut the silk ribbon into four lengths, two 1.75 m/2 yd long and two 1.25 m/ 50 in long. Thread the ribbon through the beading from corner to corner, using the bodkin. Tie the ribbon into a bow at each corner. You can work a French knot on the knot of the bow to keep it flat and in place.

Floral Garden Blanket

STITCHED BY FAY KING

This charming little blanket would be perfect for a new baby. Choose embroidery wools (DMC Tapestry Wool, Appletons Crewel Wool and overdyed wools) and silk ribbon to complement the colours in the fabric you use for the backing.

Materials

- ❧ 56 cm x 80 cm/22 in x 32 in cream blanket wool
- ❧ 1.2 m/1⅓ yd Liberty print fabric for the backing and the ruffle
- ❧ matching sewing thread
- ❧ an assortment of Piecemaker tapestry needles, sizes 18-24
- ❧ handsewing needles
- ❧ a variety of wools and silk ribbon
- ❧ 12 mm/½ in wide rayon ribbon for the bow
- ❧ tailors chalk

Method

See the Embroidery Guide and the Bow Outline on Pull Out Pattern Sheet 1.

Embroidery

1 Fold the blanket wool in half widthwise and lengthwise to find the centre. Mark this point.

2 With the tailors chalk, draw an oval, 25 cm x 46 cm/ 10 in x 18 in, centred over the middle point. Baste in the outline of the oval.

3 Embroider the flowers, using a variety of wools and silk ribbon, following the embroidery guide.

4 The posts are worked in stem stitch, using a single strand of wool. The paving is worked in large open fly stitches. It looks particularly effective when it is worked in variegated wools. (Fig. 1)

5 Make the small bows with 4 mm/¼ in wide silk ribbon. Form a loop on one side and couch it in two places. (Fig. 2). Make a matching loop on the other side. Close the centre with a straight stitch. The bow tails are straight stitch with a couple of small straight stitches worked at right angles to the tails.

6 For the large bow, tie a bow using 12 mm/½ in wide rayon ribbon. Attach the bow to the blanket, using French knots. Thread the tails of the bow through the blanket and fasten them with French knots as well.

Assembling

1 Cut six 10 cm/4 in wide strips for the ruffle across the full width of the fabric. Join the strips together to form a circle. Press the ruffle strip over double with the wrong sides together.

2 Gather the ruffle with two rows of gathering. Pull up the gathering then pin the ruffle around the right side of the embroidered blanket wool with the raw edges even. Adjust the gathering to fit. Stitch the ruffle in place, 1 cm/½ in from the blanket edge.

3 Cut the backing fabric to the same size as the embroidered blanket wool. Place the backing and the embroidered piece together with right sides facing and the raw edges even with the ruffle sandwiched in between. Stitch 1 cm/½ in from the edge, leaving a 15 cm/6 in opening in one side and taking care not to catch the fullness of the ruffle in the stitching. Turn the blanket through to the right side and slipstitch the opening closed.

4 Press the blanket on the backing side over a large fluffy towel to protect the embroidery from being pressed flat.

Fig. 1   Fig. 2

Rose Blanket

STITCHED BY MARG MANNING

Wool flower embroidery is an old favourite. What makes this blanket so unusual is the combination of this technique with the striking colour of the blanket wool, highlighted with the cream lace. We have used Appleton crewel and overdyed wools.

Materials

- ❦ 80 cm x 115 cm (32 in x 48 in) of blanket wool
- ❦ tailors chalk
- ❦ long ruler
- ❦ 8.7 m (8¾ yd) of cream insertion lace
- ❦ 90 cm (36 in) of Vyella for the backing
- ❦ embroidery wools in your chosen colours
- ❦ hand-sewing needles
- ❦ an assortment of Piecemaker tapestry needles, sizes 22 and 24
- ❦ matching sewing thread

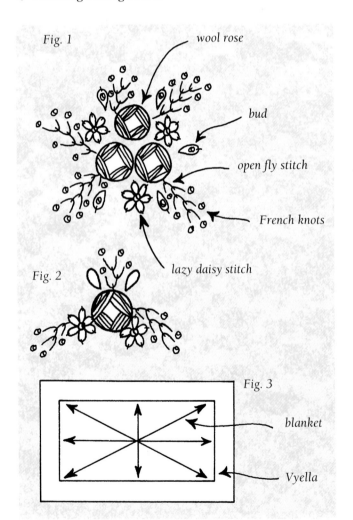

Fig. 1

wool rose

bud

open fly stitch

French knots

lazy daisy stitch

Fig. 2

Fig. 3

blanket

Vyella

Method

1 Mark diagonal lines from corner to corner on the blanket wool with the tailors chalk. Mark diagonal lines 20 cm (8 in) from the first lines.

2 Cut and pin lengths of lace along the marked lines, placing the centre of the lace on the line. Baste securely, taking care to keep the lace as straight as possible. Handsew the rows of lace into place.

Embroidery

The small bouquets (Fig. 1) are embroidered over the intersections of the lace rows with a slightly different group of flowers (Fig. 2) placed along the edges of the blanket. Following figure 1 and the stitch guide on pages 188-190, embroider three wool roses, four rose buds and three daisies in lazy daisy stitch. Work a French knot in the centre of each daisy. Work the leaves in open fly stitch with tiny French knots at the ends.

Assembling

1 Place the embroidered blanket wool in the centre of the Vyella with the wrong sides together. Trim the Vyella so that it extends 3.5 cm (1½ in) beyond the top layer all around. Securely baste the two layers together as shown in figure 3.

2 Fold the Vyella over the edge on to the embroidered blanket wool, turning under 1 cm (½ in) on the raw edge. Fold the corners into mitres. Machine-sew or hand-sew the binding into place.

3 Following figure 2, embroider the small posies around the edge of the blanket.

In an English Country Garden

EMBROIDERED BY YAN PRING

The ultimate cottage garden embroidery – complete with cottage! The lovely green of the blanket wool sets off perfectly the colours of the embroidery.

Materials

- ❧ 80 cm x 115 cm (32 in x 45 in) of bottle green blanket wool
- ❧ 4 m (4½ yd) of cream satin piping
- ❧ 140 cm (56 in) of backing fabric
- ❧ matching sewing thread
- ❧ DMC Tapestry Wool in two shades of Rose Pink
- ❧ Appleton's 2-Ply Wool, in a variety of colours
- ❧ overdyed 2-ply crewel wools
- ❧ an assortment of Piecemaker tapestry needles, sizes 18 to 24
- ❧ tailors chalk
- ❧ ruler or tape measure

Method

See the Embroidery Design on Pull Out Pattern Sheet 2.

Embroidery

1 On the wrong side of the blanket wool, mark the outline of an oval 50 cm x 30 cm (20 in x 12 in), using the tailors chalk (Fig 1). Baste around the outline and use this as your guide.

2 Following the embroidery design on the pattern sheet and the stitch guide on pages 188-190, embroider the flowers. Remember to place your flowers inside and outside the basted outline. When all the embroidery is completed, remove the basting.

Assembling

1 Lay the backing fabric face down on a table. Centre the embroidered blanket wool on the backing fabric so that the backing extends 10 cm (4 in) all around. Working from the centre, baste outwards to the four sides and the corners to hold the fabrics together securely while you work.

2 Starting at one corner, pin the piping around the blanket wool, 5 cm (2 in) from the edge, placing the piping towards the centre. Clip the seam allowance of the piping to allow you to curve it neatly around the corners. This may take up to three clips (Fig. 2).

3 Fold the backing fabric over to the blanket edge then again to meet the piping. This double fold makes a much neater finish than a simple hem. Pin the folded fabric edge to the piping, using the same pins that held the piping in place. Fold and pin the corners into neat mitres.

4 Stitch the fabric and piping in place with a blind hem stitch that catches the very edge of the fold of the backing fabric, passes through the piping and catches the blanket wool but does not stitch through the backing fabric. When you have finished stitching right around, stitch the mitres in place.

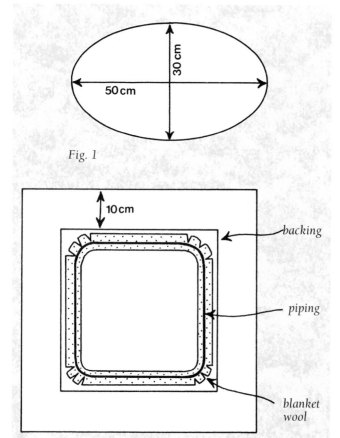

Fig. 1

Fig. 2

Bassinet Blanket

STITCHED BY MARG MANNING

A pretty fold-down top is the feature of this wool-embroidered bassinet blanket.

Materials

- ❧ 57.5 cm x 80 cm (22 in x 32 in) green blanket wool
- ❧ Appletons Crewel Wool: Green 155, Blue 742, White 991, Lilac 885, Lemon 841, Pink 943, Light Pink 752
- ❧ 5 m (5¹/₂ yd) of 4 mm (³/₁₆ in) wide silk ribbon: Pink, Light Pink
- ❧ 80 cm (32 in) Liberty print fabric for the backing
- ❧ Piecemaker tapestry needles, size 22
- ❧ Piecemaker crewel needle, size 9
- ❧ basting thread
- ❧ cotton thread to match the backing fabric
- ❧ cardboard and pencil for making the template

Method

See the Scallop Pattern and the Embroidery Designs on Pull Out Pattern Sheet 3.

For the first side

1 Measure down 10 cm (4 in) from the top edge of the blanket wool and baste a line across at this point. Mark the centre point on the line. Make a cardboard template of the scallop pattern. Using the template, baste two scallops on either side of the centre, ending 2.5 cm (1 in) from the edge (Fig. 1).

2 Work each scallop in Green feather stitch, beginning in the centre of the scallop and working up the sides. Work a White French knot at the top of each 'stem' (Fig. 2). Embroider the posies and floral sprays, following the embroidery design and the stitch guide on pages 188-190. Embroider the bows in Pink silk ribbon, catching the tails with French knots in Light Pink silk ribbon. Take the ends of the ribbon tails through to the back of your work.

Note: This embroidery is on the wrong side of the finished blanket, but will be flipped over.

For the second side

Turn the blanket over. Measure up 23 cm (9 in) from the bottom edge (the edge opposite the embroidery). Mark the scallops as before, taking care to reverse the direction (Fig. 3). Embroider the scallops and the flowers as before.

Assembling

1 Cut a 6.5 cm (2¹/₂ in) wide strip of the print fabric that is 57.5 cm (22¹/₂ in) long. Fold it in half lengthwise with the wrong sides together and press. With all the raw edges matching, stitch the strip to the top edge of the blanket (on the first side) using a 6 mm (¹/₄ in) seam. Turn the folded edge over to the other side and slipstitch it in place over the previous stitching.

2 Fold over 16 cm (6¹/₄ in) of the top edge of the blanket to the front of the blanket. Baste the edges in place. Cut the backing fabric to 70 cm x 85 cm (27¹/₂ in x 33¹/₂ in). Lay the backing fabric face down on a table. Fold under 2.5 cm (1 in) at the top edge of the backing fabric. Place the blanket, face upwards, on the backing so that the fold at the top of the blanket meets the fold on the backing and there is a 5 cm (2 in) border of the backing fabric showing around the other three sides.

3 Fold the border in half with the wrong sides together, then fold it again so that the first fold is on the blanket edge. Pin it into place. Fold each corner into a mitre. Slipstitch the edge of the border to the blanket, taking care not to stitch through the backing fabric. At the top edge of the blanket, slipstitch the two folded edges together.

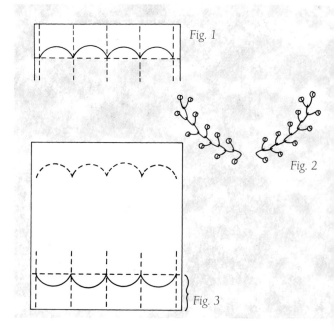

Fig. 1

Fig. 2

Fig. 3

Garden Lambs Blanket

EMBROIDERED BY GLORIA McKINNON

Baby lambs and spring flowers adorn this charming blanket, which would be a perfect project for a novice embroiderer.

Materials

- ❧ 80 cm x 115 cm (31½ in x 45 in) of blanket wool
- ❧ assortment of Piecemaker tapestry needles, sizes 20 and 22
- ❧ DMC Tapestry Wool: White, Yellow, Pale Pink, Pale Blue, Blue, Green, Black
- ❧ Appleton's Crewel Wool: Pale Pink, Pale Blue, Lemon
- ❧ 2.4 m (2⅔ yd) of Liberty fabric OR 140 cm (55 in) of another 115 cm (45 in) wide fabric for the backing
- ❧ 15 cm (6 in) of fabric for piping
- ❧ 4 m (4½ yd) of piping cord

Method

See the Embroidery Guide and Key on Pull Out Pattern Sheet 4.

1 Mark a line 45 cm (17⅔ in) from the top edge of the blanket with a row of stitches. This will be your placement guide for the top row of lambs. The second group of lambs is embroidered approximately 5 cm (2 in) below the first group.

2 Embroider the lambs and flowers, following the embroidery guide and key and figures 1 to 3.

For the piping

1 Cut five strips, each 2.5 cm (1 in) wide, across the width of the piping fabric. Cut off the selvages, then join the strips to make one long strip.

2 Fold the fabric over double, with the wrong sides together and the piping cord sandwiched in between.

3 Using the zipper foot on your sewing machine, stitch along the length of the strip, stitching as close as possible to the piping cord.

Assembling

1 Cut the backing fabric into two 1.2 m (1⅓ yd) lengths. Cut off the selvages, then rejoin the pieces down the 1.2 m (1⅓ yd) sides to achieve the required width. Press the seam open.

2 Lay the backing face down on a table. Lay the embroidered blanket on the backing, face upwards. Baste from the centre outwards to the edges and the corners to hold the whole arrangement together securely as you work.

3 Trim the backing so that it is 10 cm (4 in) bigger than the embroidered blanket all around.

4 Pin the piping to the embroidered blanket, 5 cm (2 in) from the edge. To help ease the piping around the corners, clip the seam allowance of the piping at least three times at each corner.

5 Trim the ends of the piping so that one end is 2.5 cm (1 in) longer than the other. Undo the stitching for 2.5 cm (1 in) on the longer end, pull back the fabric and cut off 2.5 cm (1 in) of the cord so that the two ends of the cord meet exactly. Fold under 1.25 cm (½ in) on the end of the fabric and place the other (shorter) end of the piping inside. Stitch the piping in place all around.

6 Fold the edge of the backing to meet the blanket, then fold it again to meet the piping. Pin the fabric in place. Carefully fold the corners into mitres, then slipstitch the backing into place, stitching through the piping and the blanket but not through the backing fabric. Stitch the mitres into place. Make sure that the machine-stitching on the piping is covered by the backing.

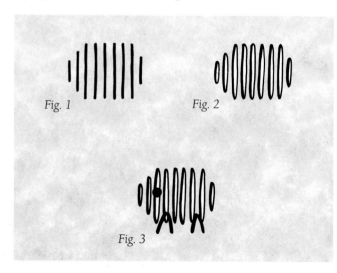

Fig. 1   *Fig. 2*

Fig. 3

Spring Blossoms

STITCHED BY CAROLINE PEARCE

Thanks to the wonderful talents of wool artist, Merilyn Ann Whalan, these blossoms are so realistic, you feel you can pick them right off the wall.

Materials

- ❧ 50 cm (19½ in) square of linen
- ❧ tracing paper
- ❧ pencil
- ❧ blue water-soluble marker pen
- ❧ Piecemaker chenille needle, size 22
- ❧ Piecemaker large tapestry needle
- ❧ Mill Hill beads Col. 02024
- ❧ Appleton's Crewel Wool: Pinks 755, 753, 143; Apricot 705; Lavender 602; Jacaranda 891, Blue 892; Yellow 851; Greens 292, 334
- ❧ Strand Embroidery Yarn, 113 OR Appleton's Crewel Wool, 894
- ❧ DMC Medici: Greens 8406, 8407
- ❧ Fancyworks 2 ply yarn: Avocado, Peach, Dusk
- ❧ Littlewood Fleece Yarns Gossamer Mohair: Claret 17, Green 6, Yellow 25
- ❧ Madeira silk thread: 1912, 2114, 1703, Black
- ❧ Madeira Decora, 1557
- ❧ Kanagawa Buttonhole Twist: 827, 114
- ❧ Waterlilies Silk 12 ply, Olive
- ❧ Mary Hart Davies overdyed silk, 3B
- ❧ DMC Stranded Cotton, 3721
- ❧ Minnamurra Stranded Cotton, 110

Method

See the Embroidery Design on Pull Out Pattern Sheet 4.

Preparation

1 Overcast or zigzag the edges of the linen to prevent them fraying.

2 Trace the embroidery design, marking the centre of the flowers and positions of the buds on the tracing. Punch a hole through the centre of each flower with a large tapestry needle and, through the hole, mark these points on the linen with the water-soluble pen. Do not transfer any more of the design to the linen at this point. Once the flowers are embroidered, draw on the stems, work the buds and leaves and the small three-petalled flowers. Finally, add the tendrils.

For the flowers

1 Each flower is composed of five petals. Using the chenille needle and the colours indicated in the chart on page 25, work three petals in the shape of a Y, then fill in the last two petals, leaving quite a large space in the centre to allow for six or seven French knots. Each petal is approximately 1 cm (³⁄₈ in) long and is made up of about seven stitches into the same holes, at the top and bottom of the petal. Place the stitches, alternately, to the right, then to the left of the first stitch. Do this by ensuring the threads are to the left of the needle for the stitch to sit on the left and to the right of the needle for the stitch to sit on the right (Figs 1 and 2). It is important to put your needle under each stitch as you pull the threads through so that the strands lie parallel and are not too tight. Space each petal so that it just touches the adjacent petal for about 3 mm (¹⁄₈ in) at the centre.

2 Work all five petals, then, using a strand of Fancyworks Avocado, work a straight stitch in between each petal, from the centre out to where the petals just separate. Tip and outline each petal with a straight stitch and a fly stitch. (Fig. 3)

3 Fill the centres of the large flowers with about seven French knots of three wraps each. Work three French knots in the centres of the periwinkles and the three-petalled yellow flowers. When you have finished the centres of the large flowers, work three straight stitches in silk on each petal beginning in the centre of the petal and converging at the centre of the flower. (Fig. 4)

4 Work the small flowers in the same way as the large ones, using a smaller initial stitch and fewer stitches in each petal. Separate the petals on the periwinkle by a straight stitch in the same colour as you used to tip the petals.

For the buds

Work the buds in the same way as the flower petals. You can vary the size of the buds by altering the length of the stitch and/or the number of stitches. First, couch the stem in place with one strand of green. Leave the thread on the right side of

the work, out of the way. Work the petal part of the bud, then add two or three straight stitches around the petal in green, working one small stitch in the centre. Work five or six small stitches in green at the base of the bud as for the petals (Fig. 5). To give extra depth to the bud, add some straight stitches in the green silk over the green wool stitches. For the base of the bud, work fly stitches with a long anchor stitch extending beyond the point of the bud. (Fig. 6)

For the leaves

1 Using the chenille needle and a single strand of Gossamer Mohair, couch the stems in place.

2 Starting at the tip of the leaf, work the leaves in fly stitch. To do this successfully, take a very uneven initial fly stitch that is quite closed. Do not anchor the stitch too close. Keep the anchor stitch fairly long so that the leaf has a nice deep V shape. If the fly stitch is too short and too open, the leaves will look like a fishbone fern. The anchor stitches make the mid rib of the leaf. If you want your leaf to curl to the right, make an uneven fly stitch so that the left side of the

stitch is much longer than the right (Fig. 7); reverse this for a leaf that curls to the left.

3 To finish the leaf, come up 2 mm ($^1/_{16}$ in) away from the base of the leaf and slide the needle under the last stitch, working from right to left, and make a smocker's knot. Anchor the knot by returning the thread to the back of the work through the stem.

For the tendrils and stems

1 Draw in some interesting lines on the linen with the water-soluble pen. Using a single strand of crewel, Medici or silk, secure the thread at the back of the work, come out on the right side of the work and lay the thread along the line, pinning it where necessary. Work tiny stitches across the thread, coming up and going down into the same hole, to secure the stem.

2 Whip the stem by going over and over the thread without piercing the fabric. Use tiny fly stitches along the stem for the thorns.

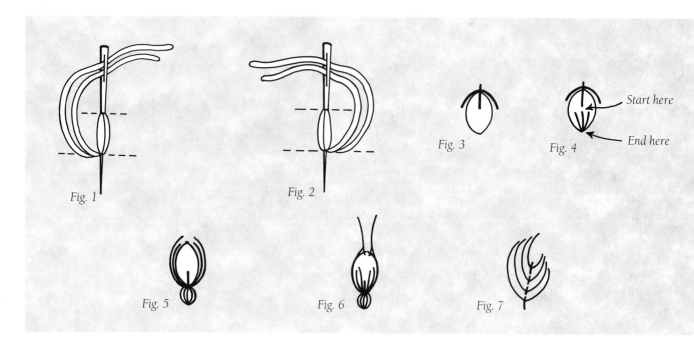

Fig. 1

Fig. 2

Fig. 3

Fig. 4

Start here

End here

Fig. 5

Fig. 6

Fig. 7

Wool Thread Chart

FLOWER	PETAL	TIPPING	CENTRE	3 STRAIGHT STITCHES
1	2 strands Gossamer Mohair Claret	1 strand Mary Hart Davies 3B	1 strand Gossamer Mohair 25 plus 1 strand Black Madeira silk	1 strand Kanagawa 114
2	2 strands Fancyworks, Dusk	1 strand Appleton's 755	as above	as above
3	1 strand each of Appleton's 755 & 143	1 strand Appleton's 602	as above Finally, stitch on beads with matching thread	
4	2 strands Appleton's 753	1 strand Appleton's 143	4 knots of the above combination & 3 knots of Fancyworks Avocado & 1 strand Madeira 2114	1 strand Decora 1557
5	2 strands Fancyworks, Peach	1 strand of the deep section of Fancyworks, Peach	as above	as above
6	2 strands Appleton's 705	1 strand Fancyworks, Peach	as above	as above
Periwinkle 7	2 strands Appleton's 891	1 strand Appleton's 892	1 strand Appleton's 851 & 1 strand Madeira 2114	
8	2 strands Appleton's 892	1 strand Strand 113	as above	
3-petalled flowers	2 strands Appleton's 851	2 strands Minnamurra 110	1 strand Kanagawa 827 & 2 strands DMC 3721	
BUD				
A	2 strands Fancyworks, Dusk	1 strand Appleton's 334		
B	2 strands Fancyworks, Dusk	1 strand Appleton's 292		
C	2 strands Fancyworks, Peach	1 strand Appleton's 292		
D	1 strand each of Fancyworks, Peach & Appleton's 705	1 strand Medici 8407, stem is whipped with Madeira 1703		
E	as above	1 strand Medici 8406, stem is whipped with Waterlilies, Olive		
F	2 strands Appleton's 705	1 strand Appleton's 334 around the bud, stem is whipped with Waterlilies, Olive		
G	2 strands Appleton's 891	1 strand Appleton's 892, stem is 1 strand Medici 8406		

Wool-embroidered Shawl

Stitched by Carolyn Hodgson

This wonderful shawl is completely reversible. The appliquéd flowers on one side cover the back of the embroidery on the other side. The flower embroidery has been designed to reflect the Hoffman fabric used in the appliqué.

Materials

- ❧ 1.5 m of 150 cm wide coloured Doctor Flannel, cut into two triangles
- ❧ a piece of fabric printed with large flowers for the appliqué
- ❧ Appletons Crewel Wool: Green 155, Tan 205, Musk 712
- ❧ DMC Broder Médici crewel wool: Purple 8895, Magenta 8101
- ❧ Danish Flower Threads, Blue/green HF226
- ❧ DMC Coton Perlé 8, 498, three balls
- ❧ Gold thread
- ❧ Mill Hill beads: Gold 02011, Antique Blue 03034
- ❧ tapestry needles, size 22
- ❧ crewel needles, size 9
- ❧ cotton thread to match the flannel
- ❧ 4 cm x 9 cm (1½ in x 3½ in) cardboard
- ❧ Vliesofix

Method

For the flowers

Embroider the flowers following the guide on page 28. The flowers are worked in buttonhole stitch, beginning at the outer petals of the flowers and working in towards the centres. Fill the centres with Gold beads, French knots in wool or with stamens worked in Gold pistol stitch.

For the appliqué

1 Choose your flowers – the appliqué will be easier if they have a definite outline. Roughly cut out the flowers.

2 Fuse the Vliesofix to the back of the flowers, then carefully cut out the flowers. Remove the paper backing, then fuse the flowers into place on the shawl, over the back of the embroidery.

For each tassel

1 Cut 2 m (2¼ yd) of Coton Perlé 8 and set it aside. This will be used later to finish off the tassel.

2 Cut another 20 cm (8 in) of the same thread and lay it along the 4 cm (1½ in) edge of the piece of cardboard. Wind the rest of your ball of thread lengthwise around the cardboard (Fig. 1).

3 With the 20 cm (8 in) of thread, securely tie off the top of the tassel and slip it off the cardboard (Fig. 2). Do not cut off the ends of this tie – they will be used to attach the tassel to the shawl.

4 Wind the 2 m (2¼ yd) length of thread around the neck of the tassel in an even band. Thread the end into a tapestry needle, work a tight backstitch over two of the bottom winds, then pass the needle into the centre of the tassel. Remove the needle. Trim the end of the tassel to an even length.

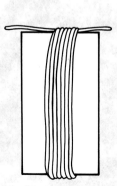

Fig. 1

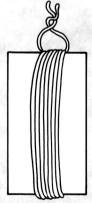

Fig. 2

Fig. 3

5 Thread some small beads onto some of the tassel strands and secure them with small knots. Decorate the top of the tassel with more beads (Fig. 3). Make three tassels.

Finishing

Fold over a corner of the shawl to the wrong side. Fold over 6 mm (¹/₄ in) on both side edges. Slipstitch the hem in place with a matching thread with a neat rolled hem. Sew a tassel in each corner.

Stitch Guide

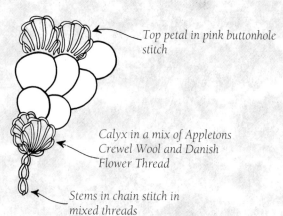

Top petal in pink buttonhole stitch

Flower petals in buttonhole stitch, starting from the outside

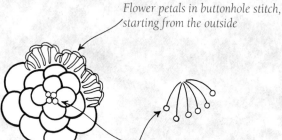

Calyx in a mix of Appletons Crewel Wool and Danish Flower Thread

Centres in pistol stitch, gold beads or French knots

Stems in chain stitch in mixed threads

Leaves in buttonhole stitch

Small purple flowers in straight stitch using two strands of wool. Sew four blue beads in the centre

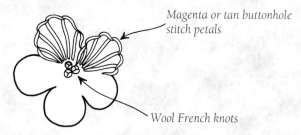

Magenta or tan buttonhole stitch petals

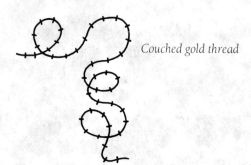

Couched gold thread

Wool French knots

Gloria's Tips
for Successful Wool Embroidery

To knot or not . . .

I use a knot because a knot gives more security to the stitches; if you prefer not to, then don't. Most wool embroidery is lined, so the back does not show.

To knot the wool, thread the needle and place the end of the thread onto the needle that is being held in the right hand. With the left hand, twist the wool four times around the needle. Holding the needle with the twists in your left hand, pull the needle through the twists with your right hand along the full length of the thread. You will then have a knot at the end.

When threading the needle, squeeze the wool between the thumb and first finger of your left hand. Holding the needle with your right hand, place the eye of the needle onto the wool, so you are threading the needle onto the wool, not the wool into the needle. Needle threaders are available, but you need a good quality one, such as the Loran needle threader, when working with wool.

If the wool becomes frayed, cut a clean end and start again.

After completing a wool flower, you can tuck the knot under the previous stitches. To end off, weave the needle and thread under two or three stitches.

Another reminder – always work with a piece of thread from finger to elbow in length. The friction of the thread going through the fabric continually frays the fibre and you will have furry stitches if your thread is too long.

Choose your lining fabric at the same time as you choose your threads so that you can incorporate the colours of the fabric into your embroidery. It is easier to match threads to fabric than fabric to threads.

Experiment with different threads, not just different plys of wool. You will enjoy the different effects, such as with the metallic threads in the shawl on page 26.

HEIRLOOM SEWING

Prized for its delicacy and beauty, fine hand-sewing has a long heritage. These days, we can achieve the hallmarks of this French style with the use of sophisticated sewing machines. Whether your preference is for the traditional hand-sewing or the new 'tradition' of machine-sewing, the allure of beautiful fabric, trimmed with lace and pintucks and worked with fine stitches, remains.

If you are a newcomer to heirloom sewing, the Church Dollies on page 32 are the perfect way to begin, giving you the opportunity to practise your skills on a sampler piece that makes up into a charming doll. For the more experienced, the Nightgown on page 34 and the Peignoir on page 39 embody the best of this style. Luxuriously trimmed with the best lace and embroidered with doves and garlands, the nightgown and peignoir set would be the perfect gift for a bride.

On a less serious note, heirloom sewing techniques have been used to fashion the charming little Angel Bunnies on page 44, and the perfect topper for your Christmas tree, the Angel on page 55.

Extravagance is the name of the game when it comes to heirloom sewing – less is definitely not more! A perfect example of this dictum is the gorgeous Chatelaine on page 48, absolutely smothered in lace and embroidery.

Church Dollies

STITCHED BY HEATHER LAMERTON

In days gone by, mothers, anxious to quieten restless children during the church service, would knot their linen hankerchiefs into a plaything.

Materials

- ❧ two pieces of fine cotton batiste,
  one 34 cm x 43 cm/13½ in x 17½ in and the other
  6 cm x 43 cm/2½ in x 17½ in for the dress and body
- ❧ 10 cm/4 in of fine cotton batiste for the collar and
  bonnet
- ❧ 1.8 m/2 yd of insertion lace
- ❧ 90 cm/36 in of beading
- ❧ 1.8 m/2 yd of entredeux
- ❧ 70 cm/28 in of edging lace
- ❧ matching sewing thread
- ❧ twin needle
- ❧ pintucking sewing machine foot (optional)
- ❧ water-soluble marker pen
- ❧ 3 mm/ ⅛ in wide ribbon
- ❧ cotton wool or polyester fibre fill
- ❧ scraps of embroidery yarns for the face and hair

Method

See the Collar Pattern on Pull Out Pattern Sheet 1.

1 Press the 6 cm x 43 cm/2½ in x 17½ in piece of batiste in half across the 6 cm/2½ in width. Using the twin needle, make the first pintuck on this fold. Make another pintuck on either side of the first one. Make another three tucks 6mm/¼ in on either side of this first group. Zigzag around the edges of the piece. (Fig. 1)

2 Cut four pieces of insertion, two pieces of beading, and four pieces of entredeux, each 43 cm/17 in long. Cut the batiste from one edge of one length of entredeux and, using a small zigzag stitch, join a piece of insertion to this edge. Next, join a length of beading to the insertion and then join a length of insertion to the beading and finally join on a piece of entredeux trimmed as before. Make two of these panels of joined lace.

3 Trim the batiste from the entredeux on the lace panels. Turn a small hem on the top and bottom of the pintucked piece. Join the trimmed entredeux to the hemmed edges of the batiste with a small zigzag stitch. (Fig. 2)

4 Gather the edging lace by pulling up a thread from the straight edge. Using a small zigzag stitch, attach the gathered edging to one of the lengths of entredeux.

5 On the larger piece zigzag along the 43 cm/17½ in edge, then turn a small hem. Attach this piece to the top edge of the joined piece, using a small zigzag stitch.

6 Round the corners slightly then roll and zigzag all the raw edges, working carefully over the laces.

To form the face

1 With the marker pen, mark the facial features in the centre of the top edge of the fabric, 9 cm/3½ in from the edge. Embroider the face, using appropriately coloured yarns.

2 Fold back approximately 7 cm/3 in at the top so that the face now sits at the top. Make a firm 5 cm/2 in ball of cotton wool or polyester fibre fill and position it behind the face. Secure the fabric around the ball by winding sewing thread around the 'neck'. Make the face and head as smooth as possible.

3 Embroider the hair with loops of embroidery yarn. Tie a knot on each side for the hands.

Collar

Cut two pieces of batiste, using the collar pattern. With right sides together, stitch around the outer edge and along the centre back edges in one continuous 3 mm/ ⅛ in seam. Turn the collar to the right side. Zigzag the raw edges together. Position the collar on the doll and catch the centre back edges together with a stitch.

Bonnet

1 Cut two pieces of batiste, one 3 cm x 4 cm/1¼ in x 1½ in and the other 2 cm x 12 cm/ ¾ in x 4¾ in. Roll and zigzag the edges of both pieces.

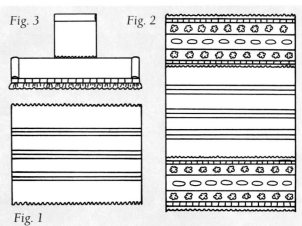

2 On the 3 cm x 4 cm/1¼ in x 1¾ in piece, make a small casing along one 4 cm/1½ in edge. Make two small casings on the 2 cm/¾ in edges of the other piece. Pin the smaller piece to the centre of one of the long sides of the larger piece then zigzag it in place (Fig. 3). Stitch a length of entredeux to the other long side.

3 Gather 24 cm/9½ in of edging lace to fit the length of the entredeux by pulling up a thread in the straight edge. Zigzag the entredeux in place.

4 Thread the silk ribbon through the casings. Pull up the ribbon and tie it in a bow under the 'chin'.

Fig. 3   Fig. 2

Fig. 1

Nightgown

MADE BY WENDY LEE RAGAN

This is a beautiful embroidered and lace-trimmed nightgown. It would also be the perfect gift for a mother-to-be as it has a generous front opening. On page 39 you will find the matching peignoir to complete the set.

Materials

- ❦ 4 m/4¼ yd of white cotton lawn for the skirt
- ❦ 60 cm/ ⅔ yd of white Swiss batiste or cotton lawn for the yoke
- ❦ 23 cm/9 in x 45 cm/18 in of light blue Swiss batiste or cotton lawn
- ❦ 2 m/2 yd of 1 cm/ ½ in wide white edging lace
- ❦ 2 m/2 yd of 2.5 cm/1 in wide white edging lace
- ❦ 2 m/2 yd of 4 cm/1½ in wide white edging lace
- ❦ 6 m/6½ yd of 5 cm/2 in wide white edging lace
- ❦ 4 m/4 yd white entredeux
- ❦ Floche embroidery thread: F20 Light Yellow, 744 Yellow, 754 Peach, 819 Light Pink, F43 Pink, 651 Light Blue, F35 Blue, 369 Green, 415 Grey
- ❦ DMC Stranded Cotton, white, for the appliqué cord
- ❦ needles, size 7 betweens
- ❦ seven small buttons
- ❦ Madeira Tanne white cotton thread, no. 80
- ❦ white sewing thread
- ❦ universal machine-sewing needles, nos 65 and 100
- ❦ no. 2 pencil or a drafting pencil
- ❦ tracing paper
- ❦ spray starch

Method

See the Pattern, Embroidery Designs and Templates on Pull Out Pattern Sheet 1.

For the yoke

1 Spray starch the white Swiss batiste or lawn fabric and press it well.

2 Trace two front yokes and two back yokes from the pattern sheet. Do not cut out these pieces but cut a rough rectangle around each shape.

3 Trace the embroidery designs from the pattern sheet and transfer the designs on to the two front yokes and one back yoke. The other back yoke piece will be the lining.

4 Embroider one left and one right front yoke, leaving the lining free. Embroider the back yoke, following the embroidery guide on the pattern sheet and the stitch guide on pages 37 and 38.

5 Wash all the yoke sections. Allow them to dry, then press well. Accurately cut out all the yoke pieces.

6 With the right sides facing, the raw edges even and using 2 cm/ ¾ in seam allowances, join the shoulder seams of the embroidered yokes. Trim the seams to 6 mm/ ¼ in and press them open. Join the shoulder seams of the front yoke linings and the back yoke lining. Trim the seams and press them open. Turn the yoke right sides out. Baste the raw neck, armhole and bottom edges together.

7 Trim the batiste from one side of the entredeux. Spray starch both the entredeux and the fabric at the bottom edge of the front and back yokes. Place the entredeux and the fabric together with right sides facing and the edge of the entredeux approximately 6 mm/ ¼ in from the fabric edge. Attach the entredeux with small zigzag stitches. Choose a stitch that places the 'zig' in the holes of the entredeux and the 'zag' in the fabric. Press the yoke and set it aside.

For the nightgown skirt

1 Cut out the following pieces:
Skirt front: 1 m/40 in x 115 cm/45 in,
Skirt back: 1 m/40 in x 115 cm/45 in, **Ruffle:** four strips 20 cm/7 in wide, cut across the full width of the fabric.

2 Trace and cut out the template for the top of the skirt pieces. Using the templates, mark the armholes for the front and back skirts. Cut out the armholes.

3 Using French seams, sew the side seams of the front and back skirts, keeping the seams 6 mm/ ¼ in or less. Press the skirt, folding the seams to the back of the garment.

4 Using a regular stitch length, sew three rows of gathering at the top of the front and back skirts. Set them aside.

5 Using tiny French seams, sew the four ruffle pieces together to form a circle. Pintuck along the centre of the ruffle, using a seven-groove pintucking foot. Place the tucks in the following grouping with a space between each group: one tuck, two tucks, three tucks, one tuck, two tucks. Press the pintucks after each tuck.

Note: You may find it easier to stitch the pintucks if you loosen the top tension slightly.

6 Attach the 5 cm/2 in wide lace edging by stitching in the heading of the lace, using a small straight stitch, then hemstitch the lace to the fabric.

Note: Use the Madeira Tanne no. 80 thread and a no. 100 universal machine sewing needle for a prettier hemstitch – more like handworked pinstitch.

7 Sew three rows of gathering at the top of the ruffle in the same way as for the top of the skirt. Gather up the ruffle to fit the bottom of the skirt, then pin and stitch the ruffle in place. Trim the seam allowance back to 6 mm/¼ in and roll and whip the raw edges.

For the front opening

1 Pull up the gathering on the top of the skirt to fit the bottom edge of the yoke. Place the entredeux and the fabric together with right sides facing, adjusting the gathering as you go, and placing the ditch of the entredeux on, or a little below, the last gathering line. Keep the area at the front where the opening placket will be free of gathering. Stitch in the ditch of the entredeux with a short straight stitch. Trim

back to 3 mm/⅛ in. Stitch with a close zigzag, stitching into one hole of the entredeux and all the way off the fabric on the other side. This will roll the fabric and entredeux edges right into the entredeux.

2 Trace and cut out the pattern for the placket. Cut out the placket from the blue Swiss batiste. Turn in and press 1 cm/½ in on the sides and bottom of the front placket, folding in the corners diagonally. (Fig. 1)

3 Pin the right side of the long side of the placket to the wrong side of the nightgown front. Stitch along the stitching lines, pivoting at the small dots. (Fig. 2)

4 Cut down the placket between the lines of stitching, clipping diagonally to the small dots. Trim the long seam allowances and press them towards the placket. (Fig. 3)

5 Fold the placket sections along the fold line with the right sides together. Stitch across the top edge and trim off the excess fabric. (Fig. 4)

6 Turn the shorter side of the placket to the outside along the fold line, placing the pressed edge over the seam. Edgestitch close to the edge, by hand or machine, ending at the small dot then stitch along the fold. Turn the other side of the placket to the outside and edgestitch as before taking care not to catch the shorter side in the seam.

7 On the outside, lap the right front band over the left front band, matching the centres. Stitch close to the edges below the small dots and along the stitching lines. (Fig. 5) Pinstitch around the front bands, if you wish.

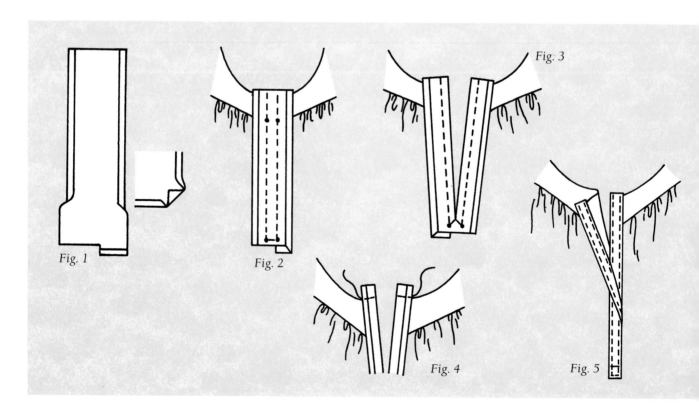

Fig. 1   Fig. 2   Fig. 3   Fig. 4   Fig. 5

8 Make seven buttonholes in the right front placket and sew on the buttons to correspond.

For the lace

1 Trim the batiste edge of the entredeux, spray starch and then sew the entredeux around the armholes as for the bottom of the yoke. Gather up the 1 cm/ $\frac{1}{2}$ in wide edging lace to fit the armholes. Sew the gathered lace to the entredeux, trim the edges and cover with a close zigzag stitch.

2 Trim and attach the entredeux and gathered lace around the neckline in the same way as for the armholes but using the 2.5 cm/1 in wide edging lace.

3 Gather the remaining 5 cm/2 in wide edging lace to fit the front yoke/skirt seam. Attach the lace by hand to the skirt edge of the entredeux with tiny stitches. Attach the lace to the back yoke in the same way, using the 4 cm/1½ in wide edging lace instead.

Stitch Guide

Shadow embroidery

Use a crewel needle, size 10, and a 45 cm/18 in single strand of stranded embroidery cotton. Place the fabric in a hoop and begin with a waste knot. In shadow stitch, you form a basketweave of thread that covers the area to be filled and is surrounded by back stitches.

1 Bring the needle through at **a** and take a stitch to **b**. Bring the needle up at **c** and take a stitch to **b**. (Fig. A)

2 Bring the needle up at **d** and take a stitch to **a**. On the wrong side, carry the thread over, bringing it out at **e** and take a stitch to **c**. (Fig. B)

3 On the wrong side, carry the thread over, bringing it out at **f** then take a stitch back to **d**. On the wrong side, carry the thread over, bringing it out at **g** then take a stitch back to **e**. Continue in this way until the area is filled. (Fig. C)

Granitos or Rondels

These are tiny dots made by laying six or seven straight stitches over one another. They can be worked with or without a hoop.

Split Stitch

This is commonly used for padding which is covered by other stitches. It can be worked with or without a hoop. (Fig. D)

Bullion Stitches

Bullion stitches are the basis for embroidering many flowers.

1 Begin by anchoring the thread, then take a stitch from **a** to **b**, taking the needle back to **a**. Insert the needle at **b** again, just up to the eye. (Fig. E)

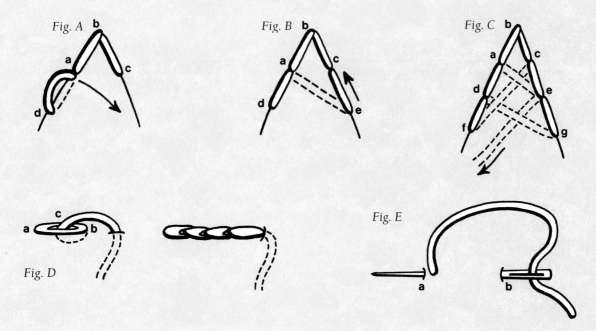

Fig. A   Fig. B   Fig. C   Fig. D   Fig. E

Stitch Guide continued …

2 Wrap the thread around the needle, keeping it close to **a**. (Fig. F). Controlling the wraps firmly with your left thumb, push the needle through and slide the wraps off the needle. Slide the wraps down the thread until they are lying on the fabric. Reinsert the needle at **b**.

Bullion rosebuds are made by laying two bullion stitches side by side. Make one of the bullions one wrap larger than the other. For a bullion rose, make three bullions side by side. The inside one is usually one or two wraps smaller than the outside ones. Here's a tip: wrap the thread around the needle until the tube is the desired length, then add one more wrap. This is to compensate for the fact that the bullion will compact when you slide it off the needle.

For bullion pinwheels, draw a circle of the desired size with a dot in the centre. Stitch around the outside with split stitches, then make bullions from the outside ring, over the split stitches, into the centre, until the circle is filled.

Shaded Eyelets

1 Draw an oval with an offset circle inside it. Outline both with split stitches. (Fig. G) With an awl, push open the threads inside the circle. Don't break the threads.

2 Inside the oval, stitch two or three layers of padding satin stitches, alternating the direction of the layers. (Fig. H)

3 When the padding is completed, satin stitch around the eyelet over the padding. These shaded eyelets can be stitched with or without a hoop. (Fig. J)

Appliqué Cord

The heart on the centre back yoke is stitched in this technique.

1 Cut a length of cord (stranded cotton) that is twice the length of the heart outline. Anchor the cord in the fabric.

2 Pinstitch over the cord until you have completed the outline of the heart. (Fig. K)

3 Bring the cord around and pinstitch over it, working back the way you came, but on the other side and using the same holes. (Fig. L)

4 To finish, overlap the cords and couch them, or bring them to the back of your work and tie them off or weave them into the stitches.

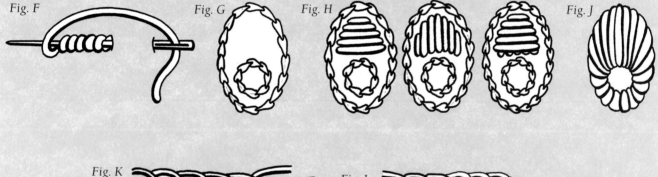

Fig. F   *Fig. G*   *Fig. H*   *Fig. J*

Fig. K

Fig. L

Peignoir

MADE BY WENDY LEE RAGAN

This elegantly embroidered peignoir is the perfect companion for the nightgown on page 34.

Materials

- ♣ 5.3 m (5¾ yd) of white cotton lawn for the skirt
- ♣ 60 cm (24 in) of white Swiss batiste or cotton lawn for the yoke
- ♣ 20 cm x 102 cm (8 in x 40 in) of light blue Swiss batiste or cotton lawn
- ♣ 1.8 m (2 yd) of 2.5 cm (1 in) wide white edging lace
- ♣ 1.8 m (2 yd) of 4 cm (1½ in) wide white edging lace
- ♣ 7.3 m (8 yd) of 5 cm (2 in) wide white edging lace
- ♣ 3.7 m (4 yd) of white entredeux
- ♣ 60 cm (24 in) of white Swiss beading
- ♣ Floche embroidery thread: F20 Light Yellow, 744 Yellow, 819 Light Pink, F43 Pink, 651 Light Blue, F35 Blue, 369 Green, White
- ♣ quilting needles, size 7 betweens
- ♣ nine small buttons
- ♣ Madeira Tanne white cotton thread, no. 80
- ♣ white sewing thread
- ♣ universal machine-sewing needles, nos 65 and 100
- ♣ 1.8 m (2 yd) of 6 mm (¼ in) wide double-sided satin ribbon
- ♣ no. 2 pencil or a drafting pencil
- ♣ tracing paper
- ♣ seven-groove pintucking foot
- ♣ spray starch

Note: Use the Madeira Tanne thread for all French machine-sewing techniques and the white sewing thread for all the simple sewing.

To gather the laces, pull up the thread in the lace heading.

Method

See the Pattern, Embroidery Designs and Templates on Pull Out Pattern Sheet 2.

1 Spray starch the white Swiss batiste or lawn fabric and press it well.

2 Trace two front yokes and two back yokes from the pattern sheet. Do not cut out these pieces but cut a rough rectangle around each shape.

3 Trace the embroidery designs from the pattern sheet and transfer the designs on to the two front yokes and one back yoke. The other back yoke piece will be the lining.

4 Embroider one left and one right front yoke, leaving the lining free, and the back yoke, following the embroidery design on the pattern sheet and the stitch guide on pages 37 and 38.

5 Wash all the yoke sections. Allow them to dry, then press them well. Accurately cut out all the yoke pieces.

6 With the right sides facing, the raw edges even and using 2 cm (¾ in) seam allowances, join the shoulder seams of the embroidered yokes. Trim the seams to 6 mm (¼ in) and press them open. Join the shoulder seams of the front yoke linings and the back yoke lining. Trim the seam and press open. Turn the yoke right sides out and press well. Baste the raw neck, armhole and bottom edges together.

7 Trim the batiste from one side of the entredeux. Spray starch both the entredeux and the fabric at the bottom edge of the front and back yokes. Place the entredeux and the fabric together with right sides facing and the edge of the entredeux approximately 6 mm (¼ in) from the fabric edge. Attach the entredeux with small zigzag stitches. Choose a stitch that places the 'zig' in the holes of the entredeux and the 'zag' in the fabric. Press the yoke again and set it aside.

For the peignoir skirt

1 From the white cotton lawn, cut out the following pieces:
Skirt fronts: two pieces 98 cm (38½ in) long and as wide as half the fabric width; **Skirt back:** one piece across the full width of the fabric that is 95 cm (37½ in) long; **Ruffle:** four pieces 28 cm (11 in) wide across the full width of the fabric.

2 From the blue Swiss batiste, cut two pieces, each 7 cm x 98 cm (2¾ in x 38½ in), for the front bands.

3 Trace the front skirt template and the armhole templates, then, using them as your pattern, cut the top edge of both front skirts and the back skirt to the appropriate shape.

4 Using French seams, sew the side seams of the front and back skirts, keeping the seams 6 mm (¼ in) or less. Press the seams towards the back.

5 Gather the top of the skirt to fit the bottom edge of the yoke. Place the entredeux and the fabric together with the right sides facing, adjusting the gathering as you go and placing the ditch of the entredeux on, or a little below, the last row of gathering. Keep the area at the front where the band will be free of gathering. Stitch in the ditch of the entredeux with small straight stitches. Trim the seam allowance back to 3 mm (⅛ in). Stitch with a close zigzag, stitching into one hole of the entredeux and all the way off the fabric on the other side. This will roll the fabric and the entredeux edges right into the entredeux.

6 Trim the batiste off two lengths of entredeux for the armhole openings. Spray them with starch, then sew the entredeux around the armholes in the same way as for the bottom of the yoke.

For the front bands

1 Mark the fold line down the middle of the bands. Turn in the seam allowance on one long edge of both bands (Fig. 1). Press, then trim the pressed seam allowance back to 1 cm (⅜ in). Sew the raw long edges of the bands to the front edges of the peignoir (Fig. 2). Trim the seam, then press the seam allowance towards the band.

2 Fold the bands along the marked fold line with the right sides together. Sew across the top edge, then trim the seam allowance. Turn the band to the right side (Fig. 3).

3 Fold the band to the inside along the fold line. Press. Slipstitch the pressed edge over the seam (Fig. 4). Baste the thicknesses together across the lower edge. Edgestitch the front of the bands and pinstitch, if you wish (Fig. 5).

For the sleeves

1 Trace the sleeve pattern for your correct length, then cut out two sleeves from the cotton lawn. Gather the top and bottom edges for the sleeves with three rows of stitches of a regular stitch length. Sew the sleeve seams with French seams, making the seams 6 mm (¼ in) or less.

2 Measure your wrist, then add 4 cm (1½ in). Gather up the ends of the sleeves to this measurement. Sew on the Swiss beading. Gather the 5 cm (2 in) wide lace, then attach it to the Swiss beading. To finish the raw ends of the lace, sew them together with a straight seam, then roll and whip the raw edges.

3 Gather the tops of the sleeves to fit the armholes, then sew the sleeves to the entredeux at the armholes.

For the ruffle

1 Using tiny French seams, sew the four ruffle pieces together to form one long strip. Press all the seams in the same direction. Narrow hem the two short ends of the strip.

2 Pintuck along the centre of the ruffle, using the seven-groove pintucking foot, making as many pintucks as you like.

Note: You may find it easier to stitch the pintucks if you loosen the top tension slightly.

3 Attach the 5 cm (2 in) wide lace edging to the bottom edge of the ruffle by stitching in the heading of the lace, using a small straight stitch, then hemstitch the lace to the fabric.

Note: Use Madeira Tanne no. 80 thread and a size 100 universal machine sewing needle for a prettier hemstitch – more like hand-worked pinstitch.

4 Sew three rows of gathering along the top edge of the ruffle in the same way as for the top of the skirt. Gather the ruffle to fit the bottom of the skirt, then pin and stitch the ruffle in place. Trim the seam allowance back to 6 mm (¼ in) and roll and whip the raw edges.

Finishing

1 Mark and sew the buttonholes on one front band and sew on the buttons to correspond.

2 Trim the batiste edge of the remaining entredeux, spray with starch, then sew the entredeux around the neckline as for the lower edge of the yoke. Gather the 2.5 cm (1 in) wide lace, then sew it to the entredeux.

3 Gather the 5 cm (2 in) wide lace, then sew it to the front yoke/skirt seam, hand-sewing the lace to the entredeux with tiny stitches. Attach the 4 cm (1½ in) wide lace to the back yoke in the same way.

4 Cut the satin ribbon in half. Thread each half through the Swiss beading on the sleeves and tie into a bow.

Option: An embroidered fancy band can be included in the design. It must be attached before the front bands are attached. Adjust the skirt length accordingly.

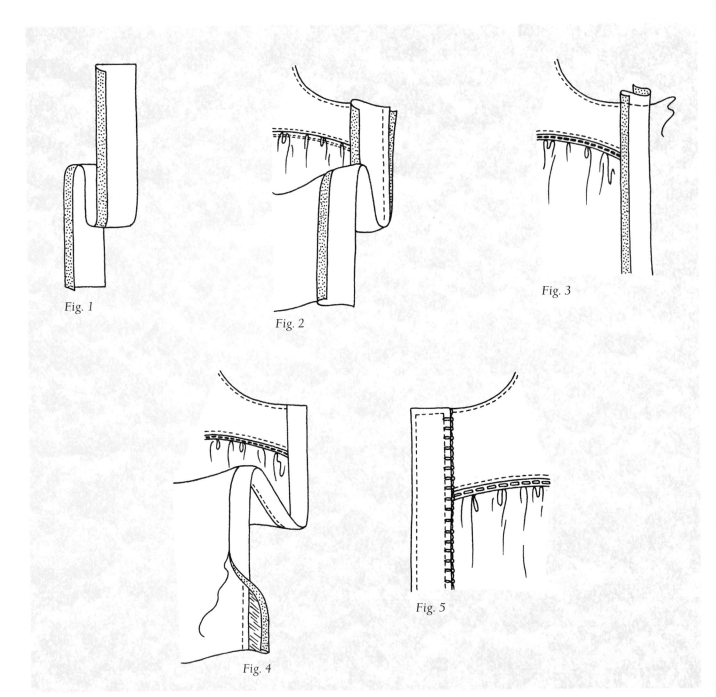

Fig. 1

Fig. 2

Fig. 3

Fig. 4

Fig. 5

Gloria's tips
for Successful Heirloom Sewing

The first and foremost rule for heirloom sewing is to use the very best quality in fabric and lace that you can afford. I always use one hundred per cent cotton fabric. It is harder to iron than a cotton/polyester mix, but it's well worth the extra effort. In addition, I always use one hundred per cent cotton thread for stitching cotton fabric and lace. French laces which are marked ninety per cent cotton and ten per cent nylon are classed as cotton laces.

If your project requires cream lace, it can sometimes be difficult to find the range of laces in cream that are available in white. I always use white lace which I dye in coffee or tea to achieve a lovely cream shade. To dye the lace: Wet the length of lace in water, then dip it in a cup of black coffee or tea. If you are happy with the colour, add two tablespoons of white vinegar to the cup and dip the lace again. The vinegar serves to set the colour. If the

colour is too light, add more tea or coffee and try again. When you have dyed like this a few times, you will be confident enough to judge the colour and add the vinegar right at the beginning, but having a trial run is a good idea until you become more confident. When you have dyed all the lace you need, allow it to dry naturally (not in the clothes dryer), then iron it. You will have beautiful ecru lace, ready for use.

Think about not using all matching laces for your sewing. I have been fortunate enough to learn from Martha Pullen, who points out that antique heirloom sewn garments mostly have three or four different laces. Susan York, another wonderful teacher, uses old lace, new lace, Swiss lace, French lace, ecru lace and white lace all together in the one garment. I have a child's dress of hers with this variety of laces and the effect is wonderful!

Angel Bunnies

<small>STITCHED BY SUSAN D. YORK</small>

These little creatures can be as simple or as elaborate as you wish to make them. We offer you a number of decorative options.

Materials

- ❧ 12 cm (5 in) purchased bunny
- ❧ 23 cm (9 in) of white batiste
- ❧ 1.8 m (2 yd) of insertion
- ❧ 2.3 m (2½ yd) of lace edging
- ❧ 15 cm x 7.5 cm (6 in x 3 in) of organdy for the wings
- ❧ 1.4 m (1½ yd) of 3 mm (⅛ in) wide ribbon
- ❧ twinkle stars
- ❧ lightweight florists wire
- ❧ matching sewing thread
- ❧ pencil
- ❧ spray starch

Method

See the Patterns, Lace-shaping Designs and the Lace Shaping Guide on Pull Out Pattern Sheet 2.

1 Cut a piece of the batiste 30 cm x 10 cm (12 in x 4 in) for the dress. At the top edge, fold over 12 cm (½ in) at the top edge and stitch a 6 mm (¼ in) casing.

2 Choose the lace-shaping design you wish to use for the hem of the dress – scallop, zigzag or heart-shaped.

Decorate the hem with the insertion, following one of the alternatives in the lace-shaping guide.

3 There are several ways you can complete the next step. Whichever method you choose, take care not to stitch through the casing. You can:

a) zigzag a length of lace edging along the stitching line of the casing. Make two 2 cm (¾ in) long slashes for the armholes (Fig. 1), then zigzag through the lace and fabric to neaten the armholes. This method will give you a lace collar effect; or

b) make the slashes as shown in figure 1, zigzag down them, then sew the lace edging along the casing stitching line. This gives the effect of a lace collar which goes across the shoulders; or

c) forget the collar effect and do not use any lace edging.

4 With the right sides together, sew the centre back seam, but do not stitch through the casing.

5 Thread a 38 cm (15 in) length of ribbon through the casing. Put the dress on the bunny and pull up the ribbon to close the neck.

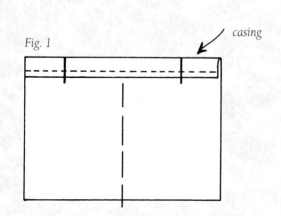

Fig. 1

casing

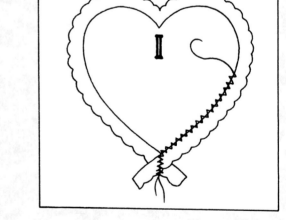

Fig. 2

For the wings

1 You will need two layers of organdy for the wings. It is best to shape the lace before you cut out the shape. Pin the two layers of organdy together, then trace the heart shape on to the organdy with the pencil.

2 Gather the lace edging by pulling up the thread in the heading. Shape the gathered lace around the heart and zigzag it into place, beginning at the bottom and letting the tails of the lace cross over (Fig. 2). Zigzag straight down the tails, then trim away the excess lace.

3 Trim the organdy to the heart shape. On the back of the wings, zigzag the white wire around the heart shape over the heading of the lace.

4 Make a tiny vertical buttonhole, approximately 3 mm (¼ in) long, at the peak of the heart, as shown in figure 2. Run the ribbon from the dress through the buttonhole and tie a bow at the back.

For the pantaloons

1 Trace the pantaloons pattern and cut out the pantaloons as directed. Stitch the centre front crotch seam.

2 Fold under 12 mm (½ in) at the top edge of the pantaloons and stitch a 6 mm (¼ in) casing.

3 Embellish the bottom edge of both legs with a row of insertion and a row of lace edging.

4 Zigzag 25 cm (10 in) of the 3 mm (⅛ in) wide ribbon around each leg, above the lace. Use a zigzag stitch that is wide enough to make a casing for the ribbon, but take care not to stitch through the ribbon. Pull out the excess ribbon in the middle so that the ends of the ribbon are even with the edges of the fabric.

5 With the right sides together, stitch the centre back seam, taking care not to stitch through the casing.

6 Fold the pantaloons so that the inner leg edges are together with the right sides facing. Stitch the seam, catching the ends of the ribbon into the seam. Cut through each loop of ribbon in the centre.

7 Thread 25 cm (10 in) of ribbon through the waist casing Place the pantaloons on the bunny, pull up all the ribbons and tie them into bows.

Chatelaine

Stitched by Wendy Lee Ragan

This exquisite embroidered chatelaine with its matching scissor case and needle case is an example of the best of the embroiderer's art.

Materials

- ❧ 60 cm (24 in) of white Irish linen
- ❧ 23 cm (9 in) square of pastel cotton velvet
- ❧ 2.75 m (3 yd) of 6 mm ($^1/_4$ in) wide white entredeux
- ❧ 2.3 m ($2^1/_2$ yd) of 1 cm ($^3/_8$ in) wide white Swiss insertion
- ❧ 1.15 m ($1^1/_4$ yd) of 5 cm (2 in) wide white lace insertion
- ❧ 5.85 m ($6^1/_3$ yd) of 4 cm ($1^1/_2$ in) wide white lace edging
- ❧ 13.4 m ($14^1/_2$ yd) of 2.5 cm (1 in) wide white lace edging
- ❧ 2 mm ($^1/_{16}$ in) wide pastel silk ribbon
- ❧ DMC Stranded Cotton: White, Ecru, Ice Blue 775, Light Yellow 746, Green 369, Yellow 744, Grey 762, Pink 776, Light Pink 818, Blue 3325
- ❧ spray-on starch
- ❧ Piecemaker between needles, size 7
- ❧ tracing paper
- ❧ sharp pencil
- ❧ transfer pencil
- ❧ 13 cm (5 in) embroidery hoop
- ❧ polyester fibre fill
- ❧ piece of felt or Doctor flannel
- ❧ cardboard or template plastic

Method

See the Embroidery Designs and the Heart Pattern on Pull Out Pattern Sheet 3.

1 Spray the linen thoroughly with the starch and press. Trace the chatelaine strip onto the linen fabric, leaving enough room to cut another strip of linen 7 cm x 103 cm ($2^3/_4$ in x $40^1/_2$ in) and a 23 cm (9 in) square of linen. (You can leave the second strip attached until after the embroidery is completed, then cut it out.) Remember to leave sufficient fabric allowance around the piece to be embroidered so that you can fit it in the hoop.

2 Using the transfer pencil, draw the embroidery designs on the strip of linen and the heart shape on the square of linen.

3 Following the embroidery designs, colour key and stitch guide on pages 37 and 38, embroider the designs on the linen. When the stitching is completed, spray and press the linen again. Cut out the two strips and set them aside.

4 Using the heart pattern, cut out one heart from the velvet. Sew a length of entredeux around the seam line. Sew a length of entredeux to the linen heart in the same way. Stitch the two hearts together by whipping the entredeux together, making two rows of entredeux and leaving a small hole for stuffing. Stuff the heart, then close the opening. You could make a heart from muslin or something similar, stuff it then slide it inside the velvet and linen heart.

5 Gather the 4 cm ($1^1/_2$ in) wide lace edging to half its length and attach it to the entredeux. Attach the narrower lace edging to the front and back of the heart. Set the heart aside.

6 Spray and press the 5 cm (2 in) wide lace insertion, then attach a length of the Swiss insertion to each long side. Pin the plain strip of linen to one side of the lace strip and the embroidered strip of linen to the other side. Fold the piece so that the embroidered linen is face down on the lace strip and the plain linen is on the bottom, under the lace. Carefully pin and baste the three pieces together. Stitch both long sides in the stitching line of the Swiss insertion, leaving the short ends open. Trim the seams and turn the piece to the right side, making sure the lace insertion is to the back, covering the linen lining. Spray and press again.

7 Fold in and baste shut the raw edges on the short ends of the piece, then attach the 6 mm ($^1/_4$ in) wide entredeux to all four sides, using a small zigzag stitch.

8 Gathering the 4 cm ($1^1/_2$ in) wide lace edging as before, stitch it to both sides of the chatelaine. Gathering the 2.5 cm (1 in) wide lace in the same way, attach it to the front and back of the chatelaine, as for the heart pillow.

9 Attach the heart pillow to one end of the chatelaine, stitching the entredeux to the velvet in the middle of the heart pillow.

10 Thread the silk ribbons through 6 mm (¹/₄ in) wide entredeux at the other end of the chatelaine and attach your scissors and other sewing needs.

Scissor Case

See the Pattern and the Embroidery Design on the Pull Out Pattern Sheet.

1 You will need to finish the embroidery before you cut out the pieces for the scissor case. Roughly cut out a square of linen just big enough to secure in the embroidery hoop. Spray the linen with the starch. Transfer the design onto the linen with the transfer pencil, then embroider the design using the stitches shown for the chatelaine.

2 When the embroidery is completed, cut two back pieces from the linen and one back piece from the cardboard or plastic. Cut off the seam allowance on the cardboard or plastic. Cut a front piece from the embroidered linen and another plain front piece. Cut one front piece from cardboard or plastic and cut off the seam allowance.

3 Sew the two back pieces together with the right sides facing, leaving an opening to insert the cardboard or plastic. Turn to the right side, slip the cardboard or plastic inside and slipstitch the opening closed.

4 Make the front piece in the same way as the back piece. Gather 15 cm (5⁷/₈ in) of the 2.5 cm (1 in) wide lace edging to half this length. Slipstitch the lace to 7.5 cm (3 in) of entredeux, then slipstitch the other edge of the entredeux to the top edge of the front piece.

5 Place the front piece on the back piece with right sides facing upwards and the bottom and side edges matching. Slipstitch them together around the side and bottom edges.

6 Gather 72 cm (28³/₈ in) of the 2.5 cm (1 in) wide lace edging. Stitch the lace to one edge of sufficient entredeux to go around the outside edge of the scissor case – approximately 36 cm (14¹/₄ in). Slipstitch the other edge of the entredeux around the entire edge of the scissor case.

7 Make a twisted cord from lengths of embroidery thread and attach the ends to the back of the scissor case, leaving a loop for hanging.

Needle Case

See the Pattern and the Embroidery Design on the Pull out Pattern Sheet.

1 Roughly cut out a square of linen big enough to secure in the hoop. Work as for step one of the scissor case.

2 Cut out two pieces of linen for the outer (embroidered) and inner (plain) layers. Cut out one piece from the cardboard or plastic and cut off the seam allowance.

3 Place the inner and outer layers together with the right sides facing and the raw edges matching. Sew around the edge, leaving one short end open. Turn to the right side, slip the cardboard or plastic into the case and slipstitch the opening closed.

4 Gather 76 cm (30 in) of 2.5 cm (1 in) wide lace edging to half this length. Slipstitch the gathered lace to sufficient entredeux to go around the outside of the needle case. Slipstitch the other edge of the entredeux to the edge of the needle case.

5 Cut four pieces of felt or flannel with pinking shears. Layer them one on top of the other, then centre them on the inside of the needle case. Stitch the felt or flannel in place using a small satin stitch down the spine.

6 Make a twisted cord from lengths of embroidery thread. Slipstitch the cord to the spine of the needle case. Thread lengths of silk ribbon through the entredeux in the centre of the short ends of the needle case to tie into a bow.

Christening Gown Pillowcase

MADE BY WENDY LEE RAGAN WITH THANKS TO MARGARET BOYLES

This beautiful lace-trimmed pillowcase is definitely a family heirloom in the making.

Fits a pillow: 51 cm (20 in) wide

Materials

- ♣ 1 m (1⅛ yd) of linen or Swiss batiste
- ♣ 4.75 m (5¼ yd) of lace (linen) tape, pale pink
- ♣ 3 m (3¼ yd) of lace insertion, number 1
- ♣ 2 m (2¼ yd) of lace insertion, number 2
- ♣ 2.1 m (2⅓ yd) of lace insertion, number 3 (optional)
- ♣ 4.8 m (5⅓ yd) of lace edging
- ♣ 2.4 m (2⅔ yd) of entredeux
- ♣ Floche embroidery thread in your chosen colours for the flower embroidery
- ♣ Piecemaker between needles, size 7
- ♣ Madeira Tanne cotton thread, no. 80, white
- ♣ ribbon for the beading and the eyelets
- ♣ spray starch
- ♣ water-soluble marker pen OR an HB, 2H or 3H pencil

For the optional flounced inner pillowcase

- ♣ 1 m (1⅛ yd) of Swiss batiste, white
- ♣ 1 m (1⅛ yd) of Swiss batiste, pale pink
- ♣ 4.5 m (5 yd) of lace edging
- ♣ 1.2 m (1⅓ yd) of 4 cm (1½ in) wide Swiss beading

Method

See the Pattern, Embroidery Design and Monogram on Pull Out Pattern Sheet 4 and on page 54.

1 Pull threads on the edges of the linen to even them off. Spray the linen with starch and press it well.

2 Trace the oval embroidery design from page 54 and the monogram from the pattern sheet onto the linen. Embroider the design in the stitches indicated, following the stitch guide on pages 37 and 38. Do not embroider the feather stitch until after the lace and tape are pinstitched into place. Using a stiletto or something similar, make the two small eyelet holes in the oval. Stitch around the holes with fine buttonhole stitches. When the embroidery is completed, press the linen again, using a well-padded ironing board and a pressing cloth.

3 Curve, shape and mitre the lace tape, then baste it into place by hand as indicated on the pattern.

4 Baste by hand as many rows of the optional lace insertions as you wish. Carefully spray the piece with starch and press again with a medium iron setting.

5 Pinstitch the lace and tape into place. Work the feather stitch embroidery. When all the lace is applied and the embroidery completed, cut away the linen from behind the lace insertion, but not from behind the lace tape.

6 Join the side seam of the pillowcase, using a French seam. Sew the top of the pillowcase with a French seam.

7 Attach the entredeux to the scallops and points on the bottom edge of the pillowcase.

8 Carefully wash the pillowcase to remove all marker pen or pencil marks, then press it while it is still slightly damp, using the padded ironing board and the pressing cloth.

9 Gather the lace edging and stitch it to the entredeux at the bottom of the pillowcase. Roll and whip the raw edge of the lace edging. Insert the ribbon.

For the flounced inner pillowcase

1 Repeat step 1 for the pillowcase. Fold the batiste over double, then join the sides and one end with French seams, leaving one end open. Attach Swiss beading to the open end of the pillowcase.

2 On the pale pink Swiss batiste, pull threads to even the edges, then cut two pieces, each approximately 46 cm x 112 cm (18 in x 44 in). Join them with a French seam to form a piece approximately 46 cm x 224 cm (18 in x 88 in).

3 Draw scallops along one long edge of the pink batiste. Shape and baste the lace edging along the scallops. French seam the short ends closed, forming a loop. Pinstitch the lace edging to the pink batiste. Cut away the fabric from behind the lace edging.

4 At the straight end of the pink batiste, run three rows of gathering thread, using a regular stitch length. Pull up the gathering to fit the Swiss beading on the end of the pillowcase. Pin, then stitch the gathered edge to the beading. Run ribbon through the beading. Press the pillowcase and flounce carefully.

Shaded eyelet

Shadow embroidery

Bullion rose

Granitos

Bullion pinwheel

Lazy daisy stitch

Bullion rosebud

Buttonhole stitch

Angel

STITCHED BY SUSAN D. YORK

Make this perfect angel for the top of your Christmas tree, or for any other time you want a pretty companion with charm and style.

Materials

- ♣ 23 cm (9 in) of cream or flesh-coloured fabric for the body
- ♣ 30 cm (12 in) of white batiste or organdy for the dress
- ♣ 4.1 m (4¹/₂ yd) of insertion
- ♣ 5.5 m (6 yd) of lace edging
- ♣ 2.75 m (3 yd) of 3 mm (¹/₈ in) wide ribbon
- ♣ 12.5 cm x 25 cm (5 in x 10 in) of organdy for the wings
- ♣ lightweight florists wire for the arms
- ♣ white lightweight florists wire for the wings
- ♣ mini curls
- ♣ twinkle stars
- ♣ polyester fibre fill
- ♣ acrylic paints and powder blusher make-up for the face
- ♣ fine paintbrush
- ♣ pencil
- ♣ tracing paper
- ♣ matching sewing thread

Method

See the Patterns and the Lace Shaping Guide on Pull Out Pattern Sheet 3.

1 Cut out the body parts as directed from the cream or flesh-coloured fabric.

2 From the white fabric, cut out a piece, 23 cm x 56 cm (9 in x 22 in), for the dress and, using the patterns on the pattern sheet, cut out the pieces for the pantaloons and the sleeve.

3 Place the body sections together with the right sides facing. Sew around the outside edge in a 6 mm (¹/₄ in) seam, using a very small stitch (stitch length 2.0) and leaving the bottom edge open. Join the legs in the same way, leaving the top edge open. Turn the legs and body to the right side. Stuff them firmly with the fibre fill, leaving enough room unfilled at the top of the legs and the bottom of the body to attach them. Place the top edge of the legs inside the body so that the toes are pointing forward. Turn in 6 mm (¹/₄ in) on

the bottom edge of the body and slipstitch the opening closed.

4 Embellish the ends of the sleeve with insertion and lace edging. Zigzag over 20 cm (8 in) of ribbon across the ends of the sleeve, forming a casing for the ribbon and taking care not to catch the ribbon in the stitching. Pull up the ribbon in the centre of both sleeve ends so that there is a loop in the middle and the ends of the ribbon protrude 1.2 cm (¹/₂ in) beyond the edge of the fabric (Fig. 1). Fold the sleeve over double, lengthwise, with the right sides together and sew a 6 mm (¹/₄ in) seam down the long side, forming a tube and catching the ends of the ribbon in the seam. Turn the sleeve through to the right side. Cut the loop of ribbon in the middle (Fig. 2).

5 Fold the arm piece over double, lengthwise, with the right sides together. Sew the long side with a 6 mm (¹/₄ in) seam, forming a tube. Turn the arm through to the right side. Pass a piece of the lightweight wire into the tube. Tie a knot in the middle of the arm to simulate clasped hands. Place the arm inside the sleeve so that the knot is inside and the raw ends of the arm are exposed at the open ends of the sleeve. Overlap the ends of the arm, including the wire, and stitch them together in a 6 mm (¹/₄ in) seam. Rearrange the arm so that the knot (hands) sits at the front, between the sleeve ends. Pull up the ribbons to gather the sleeve ends around the wrists.

6 Choose the lace-shaping design you wish to use to embellish the hem of the dress – scallop or zigzag. Working on the right side of the fabric, apply the lace in your chosen design.

7 Working on the wrong side of the top edge of the dress, stitch on a length of lace edging for the collar. When the collar is flipped over onto the front of the dress, this will be the right side. Fold 4 cm (1¹/₂ in) on the top edge over to the right side and stitch a 6 mm (¹/₄ in) casing. Sew the centre back seam, taking care not to stitch over the casing. Thread 30 cm (12 in) of ribbon through the casing. Place the dress on the angel, pull up the ribbon around the neck, tie a knot, then use the tails of the ribbon to tie the arm/sleeve to the back of the angel.

For the wings

1 You will need two layers of organdy for the wings. It is best to shape the lace before you cut out the shape. Pin the two layers of organdy together, then trace the heart shape on to the organdy with the pencil.

2 Gather the lace edging by pulling up the thread in the heading. Shape the gathered lace around the heart and zigzag it into place, beginning at the bottom and letting the tails of the lace cross over (Fig. 3). Add a second row of lace. Zigzag straight down the tails, then trim away the excess lace.

3 Trim the organdy to the heart shape. On the back of the wings, zigzag the white wire around the heart shape over the heading of the lace.

4 Make a tiny vertical buttonhole – approximately 3 mm (¹/₄ in) – at the peak of the heart, as shown in figure 3. Run the ribbon from the dress through the buttonhole and tie a bow at the back.

For the pantaloons

1 Cut out the pattern pieces as instructed. Stitch the centre front crotch seam.

2 Fold under 1.2 cm (¹/₂ in) at the top edge of the pantaloons and stitch a 6 mm (¹/₄ in) casing.

3 Embellish the bottom edge of both legs with a row of lace edging.

4 Zigzag 25 cm (10 in) of the 3 mm (¹/₈ in) wide ribbon around each leg, above the lace. Use a zigzag stitch that is wide enough to make a casing for the ribbon, but take care not to stitch through the ribbon. Pull out the excess ribbon in the middle so that the ends of the ribbon protrude 1.2 cm (¹/₂ in) beyond the edges of the fabric.

5 With the right sides together, stitch the centre back seam, taking care not to stitch through the casing.

6 Fold the pantaloons so that the inner leg edges are together with the right sides facing. Stitch the seam, catching the ends of the ribbon into the seam. Cut through each loop of ribbon in the centre.

7 Thread 25 cm (10 in) of ribbon through the waist casing. Place the pantaloons on the angel, pull up all the ribbons and tie them into bows.

For the hair and face

1 Attach rows of mini curls to cover the head. Make and attach a halo from the twinkle stars.

2 With the paintbrush, paint in the features with the acrylic paints. Dip your finger in the blusher and just touch it to the cheeks. Use a very light touch.

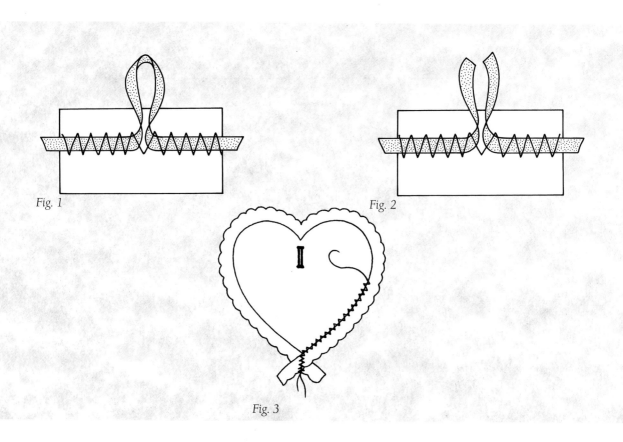

Fig. 1

Fig. 2

Fig. 3

FOLK ART AND PAPER TOLE

Deep within us all lurks the ambition to be an artist, to create objects of beauty. Unfortunately, not all of us have the talent to achieve this ambition. Folk art and paper tole are two crafts which bridge the gap between our ambitions and our skills. Any one of us really can produce a wonderful piece that we can exhibit to friends and family with great pride – and without exceptional talent.

Folk art has always been associated with the aspirations of ordinary folk to create objects of beauty in their everyday lives. As a result, from the Middle Ages to the Industrial Revolution, European peasant women devoted precious time to painting utensils and containers for special occasions, decorating the home with symbols of fertility and abundance.

In these frenetic times, it is reassuring to look back at a less complicated era with its simple pleasures, and folk art is one way we can do this. The Painted Birdhouse on page 60 has a delightfully naive feel with its transformation into a barn complete with silo, quilt, birds and flowers. If you like the design, but don't want a birdhouse, you could paint any one of the designs on any flat surface, such as a box, a tray or a wall plaque. The Painted Lamp on page 67 shows a more sophisticated design, though it still retains the simplicity of folk art painting.

Paper tole is another traditional craft enjoying a revival. With some simple tools you probably have at home already – and a little patience – you can create these delightful three-dimensional images. The two examples in this chapter show the effect you can achieve from the cutting and layering of a set of prints, specially produced for paper tole.

Painted Birdhouse

PAINTED BY PIECEMAKERS COUNTRY STORE, CALIFORNIA

Welcome the birds to your garden with this wooden birdhouse, painted in the primitive style.

Materials

- ❦ wooden birdhouse and silo
- ❦ sponge brush, size 2.5 cm (1 in)
- ❦ shader brushes, size 4 and size 10 or 12
- ❦ liner brush, size 2
- ❦ disposable sponge brush or old brush for staining
- ❦ stencil brush, size 1 cm (³/₈ in) or an old brush
- ❦ four sheets of tracing paper, 23 cm x 30 cm (9 in x 12 in)
- ❦ one sheet of palette paper
- ❦ one sheet of sandpaper, medium to fine
- ❦ one sheet of transfer paper, white
- ❦ one sheet of graphite paper
- ❦ stylus
- ❦ sharp pencil
- ❦ masking tape
- ❦ Pigma pen, black, size .01
- ❦ matt clear varnish, water-based, either spray-on or brush-on, if the birdhouse is to be indoors. If outdoors, use a non-yellowing, polyurethane varnish.
- ❦ liquid wood stain, Fruitwood
- ❦ wood glue
- ❦ paper towel
- ❦ Jo Sonja Colors: Nimbus Gray, Red Earth, Warm White, French Blue and Teal, Turners Yellow, Indian Red Oxide, Storm Blue, Pine Green, Jade, Black and two or three other colours for the hearts on the quilt and the wildflowers
- ❦ FolkArt Acrylic Sealer

Method

See the Painting Designs on Pull Out Pattern Sheet 3.

Note: Unless specified otherwise, use a brush and transfer paper appropriate to the area you are working on.

Preparation

1 Spray the birdhouse and silo lightly with two coats of sealer, following the manufacturer's instructions. Allow the sealer to dry between coats, but do not sand at this time.

2 Using the sharp pencil, trace the painting design for each side of the birdhouse onto a separate sheet of tracing paper. Trace every detail. The broken lines indicate that you will be painting that area after the basecoating is completed.

Painting

1 Using the sponge brush or the size 10 or 12 shader brush, basecoat all four sides of the birdhouse with Warm White. Paint the roof and the base with French Blue and Teal. Take care to paint with long even strokes in the direction of the wood grain. When this paint is completely dry, run a strip of masking tape around three sides of the base and the front flat portion of the base to keep that area free of other paint while you work.

2 Paint the silo with Red Earth and the attached block in Warm White. Paint the base of the silo in French Blue and Teal.

3 Using the stylus and the graphite paper, transfer the tree trunk and branches onto the back of the birdhouse. Paint the tree trunk with Indian Red Oxide. Transfer the rest of the design, but not the dotted details as you will be painting over these when you basecoat. Transfer the fence around both sides of the block behind the silo. Do not transfer the V-shaped detail on the barn door, tree foliage, wild flowers, grass and the apple basket. When transferring the sunflowers, you need only indicate their position with a dot.

4 Using the size 4 shader brush, paint the fence Nimbus Gray. Using the size 10 or 12 shader brush, paint the barn door (not the trim) in Red Earth. Using the same colour and the size 4 shader brush paint the heart and the apples sign. Using French Blue and Teal, and the same brush, paint the welcome sign.

5 Using the liner brush, paint the horseshoe in Indian Red Oxide and the border of the apples sign in French Blue and Teal.

6 Using the size 4 shader brush, paint the sunflower sign in Storm Blue. When the paint is dry, transfer the sunflower

and letters onto the sign, using the white transfer paper. Paint the sunflower in Turners Yellow, and paint the letters in Warm White, using the size 2 liner brush. Stipple the centre of the sunflower with Indian Red Oxide. Dab small dots or stipple Black around the edges of the sunflower centre. Paint the lines on the petals with Indian Red Oxide, starting from the centre and working outwards.

7 Paint the centre of the quilt in Warm White and the border around the quilt and the quilt tabs in Storm Blue. Paint the rod and the hearts on the ends in Red Earth. Transfer the quilting stitches, using the stylus and graphite paper. Paint the hearts in the colours of your choice. When the paint is completely dry, draw in the quilting stitches, using the black Pigma pen.

8 Paint the crows Black. Dip the small end of the stylus into Turners Yellow and dot the eye. When the dot dries, paint a smaller black dot in the centre of the yellow one.

9 Transfer the apple basket and the apples. Paint the basket Indian Red Oxide and the apples Red Earth. To add detail, transfer the shape of the individual apples, then outline them in a darkened red.

10 Paint the stems and leaves of the sunflowers in Pine Green. Paint each sunflower one at a time as follows: With the end of your largest brush and Turners Yellow, paint a dot on the stem where the flower head is to sit. This dot will be the size of the flower centre. Immediately, using the stylus,

move the paint outwards from the centre, just enough to create the appearance of petals. Practise a few times on paper until you get the effect you want. When the sunflowers are dry, dot the centre of each flower with Indian Red Oxide, using the liner brush. To increase the size of the centre, twist the brush in a circular motion until you have an appropriate sized centre.

11 Stipple the foliage on the apple tree, using the stencil brush or the old brush. Pour a small quantity of light, medium and dark green paint onto the palette paper. Load the brush with the two darker greens, then pounce the brush up and down on a paper towel to remove much of the paint. Now, pounce the brush up and down where you want the foliage to be. Don't clean the brush in water but wipe it off with a paper towel, then stipple in the same way, using the light green paint. Again, practising the technique on paper first is a good idea. When the foliage on the tree is dry, paint in the apples.

12 Stipple grass around all four sides of the birdhouse, except in front of the barn door, using all shades of green and taking care to make the grass quite irregular.

13 The flowers are quite easy to paint, so relax and have fun with them. Using the colours of your choice and the end of your stylus, paint four dots to suggest the petals of a flower. Paint a contrasting dot in the centre. Use fresh paint for every couple of dots.

Front

Side

Finishing

1 When all the paint is completely dry, it is time to sand your birdhouse to give it that time-worn look. Cut the sheet of sandpaper into quarters. Fold each quarter in half and sand in the direction of the wood grain, beginning with the roof, then the sides, then the base, then the silo. Sand as much as you like until you have an effect that pleases you. Be careful not to sand away more details than you intend to.

2 Before staining, wipe away all the sawdust. Apply the stain with the disposable sponge brush or old paint brush. Stain the roof first, then the sides and base. Wipe off the stain, then stain the silo.

3 Leave the birdhouse to dry for twenty-four hours before attaching the silo to the side of the birdhouse with the wood glue. Finally, varnish the whole birdhouse and silo with the appropriate varnish.

Back

Paper Tole Nursery

MADE BY LISEL HEEPS

This paper tole picture shows the craft at its most charming. You don't need great skill – just a little patience.

Materials

- ❧ five prints of the picture
- ❧ cardboard for the backing board
- ❧ craft knife or scalpel
- ❧ spray adhesive
- ❧ tube of silicone
- ❧ self-healing cutting mat
- ❧ length of grey thread
- ❧ matchsticks
- ❧ tweezers
- ❧ toothpicks
- ❧ craft glue

Method

Note: Cut-out elements are shaped before being attached, to give them a more realistic appearance. To shape, place the cut-out piece in the palm of your cupped hand and roll the scalpel handle or other cylindrical object across it. Use the tweezers to handle the cut-out pieces.

Sheet 1

Spray the back of one complete print with the spray adhesive and stick it onto the backing board.

Sheet 2

1 Using the craft knife or scalpel and the cutting mat, cut out the frame around the picture, including the flowers and the rabbits in the corners. Cut away all the background in the middle of the print, cutting around the curtains, the cat and the bassinet. Cut away and discard the wall, leaving the vines and flowers around the window as shown.

2 Using small blobs of silicone on the end of a toothpick, attach what remains of the picture to the backing picture you have already stuck down. Place the silicone at regular intervals and take care to use only small amounts of silicone to attach the frame, the corner flowers and the rabbits.

Sheet 3

1 Cut out the windows, the arch over the windows and the printed side of the curtains, cutting through the balcony railing as shown. Cut the cane edge of the bassinet, the toy rabbit, the toy horse and the pillow in the bassinet. Set all of these pieces aside. Cut out and discard all window panes.

2 Attach the vine and the archway, using small blobs of silicone at regular intervals. Attach the windows, taking care not to use too much silicone. Where you have cut the curtain overlap from the window, use a little more silicone to raise the curtain up slightly higher than the window. Use a small amount of silicone to attach the bassinet piece.

3 Stick on a piece of grey thread for the string on the toy horse, then attach the toy horse.

4 Make a small cut between each brick above the right-hand window, then put a small amount of silicone under the top edge of each brick so the bricks stand away slightly.

Sheet 4

1 Cut out the baby's suit from the window, the door handles, the cat, the balcony railings and the front edge of the balcony floor. Set these pieces aside. Discard the rest.

2 Using only very small amounts of silicone, attach all of these small pieces.

Sheet 5

1 Cut out the cat, the flower pot, the vines that creep over the balcony railings, and the vines over the archway. Set these pieces aside and discard the rest.

2 Attach all the pieces carefully with small amounts of silicone.

Finishing

As the picture already has a high gloss, glazing is optional. When you are satisfied with your picture, have it framed.

Sheet 1 and Sheet 2

Sheet 3

Sheet 4

 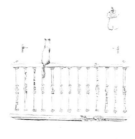

Sheet 5

Painted Lamp

PAINTED BY MEROPE MILLS

This lovely folk art painted lampstand and shade will find a place in any home. Choose colours to suit your own decor or follow the colour and painting instructions given here.

Merope recommends that you buy the shade unassembled at a store which makes lampshades. Work on it flat, then when the painting is completed, return the shade to the store to be assembled.

Materials

- ♣ laminated paper lampshade
- ♣ lampstand with an electrical fitting
- ♣ graphite paper, white and blue
- ♣ stylus
- ♣ coloured chalk pencil
- ♣ tape measure
- ♣ large and small sea sponges
- ♣ flat brush, size 2.5 cm/1 in
- ♣ Raphael S8404 brush, size 2 or 3
- ♣ old plate or saucer for a palette
- ♣ Jo Sonja All-Purpose Sealer or another water-based sealer
- ♣ Jo Sonja Colors: Warm White, Teal Green, Smoked Pearl, Fawn, Burgundy, Plum Pink, Red Earth
- ♣ Matisse Professional Artists Acrylic Colour, Antique Green OR Jo Sonja Colors, Teal Green mixed with Fawn
- ♣ clear satin-proof varnish

Method

See the Painting Designs on Pull Out Pattern Sheet 1.

Lampshade

Note: The right side of the shade is the shiny side.

1 Mix together Antique Green and Smoked Pearl to make a pale green. Add a little water to the mixture.

2 Wet the larger sponge and squeeze out any excess water. Dip the sponge into the paint and sponge the shade on the right side from one side to the other. Leave it to dry, then sponge the back of the shade. Leave it to dry.

3 On the right side, measure 6.5 cm/2¾ in from the bottom edge of the shade. Mark a line, using the chalk pencil, all the way around to the other end.

4 Using the 2.5 cm/1 in flat brush, paint the border in Antique Green. Leave it to dry, then apply a second, then a third coat – leaving it to dry between coats. Test the border to make sure it is opaque and not streaky by holding it in front of a switched-on light bulb. If there are any streaks, apply another coat.

5 Where the border meets the sponged part of the lampshade, paint in a scalloped border in Warm White.

For the leaves

1 Trace the leaf design from the Pattern Sheet on to the Antique Green border using the white graphite paper and a stylus. Use the coloured graphite paper for the leaves which go beyond the border into the sponged section. Repeat the design along the shade, making four clusters of leaves.

2 Using the size 2 or 3 brush, paint the leaves in a mixture of Teal Green and Antique Green, making them darker than the border. Paint them from top to bottom with smooth, regular strokes until you have covered the entire leaf. Paint the veins and detail of the leaves in Teal Green.

For the flowers

1 Trace in the large flowers in the same way as for the leaves. Do not trace in the daisies. Base coat the large flowers in Smoked Pearl, blocking out the leaves. If required, apply a second coat after the first coat is dry. Take care that the painting is smooth and has no ridges. Trace in the detail of the individual petals and centres.

2 The flowers are painted in the three following colour mixes and you can alternate the colours in each posy:
First colour: a mixture of Plum Pink and Fawn, with a touch of Warm White. The centre is Burgundy.
Second colour: a mixture of Red Earth and Fawn, with a touch of Warm White. The centre is Red Earth.
Third colour: a mixture of Smoked Pearl, with a touch of Fawn. The centre is Burgundy.

Paint the centre flower in the first posy in the first colour, paint the flowers left and right of the centre flower in the second colour, then paint the flower on the far right side in the third colour.

3 Squeeze out Warm White on to your palette. Load the size 2 or 3 brush with thick Warm White, flattening the brush in the paint. Carefully pull the paint down towards the centre of the flower, working from the outer edge of each petal. Clean your brush and gently blend in the white by smudging the paint where the two colours meet. Repeat the process for the bottom petals.

4 Paint in the appropriate colour for the centre and again blend where the two colours meet.

5 Paint in the stamens which fan out, then add little white dots at the end of each one.

For the daisies

1 Paint the daisies in a mixture of Fawn and Warm White. You can paint these freehand, referring to the design for positioning.

2 Twirl the brush into a point in the paint. Pick up a dot of paint and pull little commas straight into the centre, working in a circle to form the daisy. Add a Red Earth dot for the centre. Outline the petals in Warm White. Add trailing sprigs. Paint commas to represent buds in shades of Fawn, Red Earth and Warm White. Allow to dry thoroughly.

Finishing

Wet the small sea sponge and squeeze out all the water. Squeeze the sealer out on to a palette. Dip the sponge into the sealer and work with even movements from the top of the shade to the bottom and from one end to the other on the right side of the shade. When the sealer is dry, apply a second coat, leave it to dry, then apply a third coat. Seal the back of the shade with two coats of sealer.

Lampstand

Repeat the posy twice on the bottom of the stand and paint it in the same way as the lampshade. Varnish the stand with two coats of clear varnish.

If you would like some additional information about Merope's style of painting, the following books might be useful:

❧ *Imaginative Brushwork*, Milner Craft Series
❧ *Victorian Lace & Roses*, Heirloom Project
   (Elladvent Pty Limited
❧ *Hollyhock Cottage*, Heirloom Project
   (Elladvent Pty Limited)

Paper Tole Picture

MADE BY GLORIA McKINNON

Paper tole is a traditional craft which is currently enjoying a great revival. Different elements are cut out of identical pictures and are then layered to give a realistic three-dimensional effect.

This really is a project anyone can do and the results will be enjoyed for years to come.

It is a good idea to have your picture professionally framed to give it a perfect finishing touch.

Materials

- ❧ six Mollie Brett Nursery Rhyme Prints
- ❧ craft knife or scalpel
- ❧ self-healing cutting mat
- ❧ 20 cm x 24 cm/8 in x 9½ in backing board
- ❧ tube of silicone
- ❧ pencil
- ❧ tweezers
- ❧ toothpicks
- ❧ spray adhesive
- ❧ hi-gloss varnish and thinner
- ❧ small brush
- ❧ Faber Castell Studio Marker, grey

Method

Note: Pieces are shaped before being attached, to give them a more realistic look. To shape, place the cut-out piece in your cupped hand and roll the scalpel handle or another cylindrical object across it.

On the backing board, draw a circle the same size as the picture, leaving a 4.5 cm/1¾ in space at the top.

Sheet 1

1 Using the craft knife or scalpel and the cutting mat, cut out the upper oven, including the rabbit's head; the lower oven, including the dough; and the doorway. Place the remainder of the picture on the circle on the backing board and lightly mark the positions of the cut-out pieces with the pencil. Set this part of the picture aside – it could be useful later if you make a mistake with another part.

2 Glue the cut-out pieces accurately into position using the spray adhesive. Use the tweezers and the toothpicks to help you position the pieces.

Sheet 2

1 Cut out the upper oven again, but this time do not include the rabbit's head; cut out the lower oven again, excluding the dough; and cut out the doorway again.

2 On the part of the picture that remains, shape the door frame and the oven opening slightly inwards to give added dimension to the oven and door. Glue it in place over the stuck-down pieces on the backing, using the spray adhesive. Take care not to flatten the shaping.

Sheet 3

1 Cut around the baker's shovel, the table legs, the bread and tray and all four rabbits in one piece. Colour all the cut edges with the marker pen.

2 Attach the baker's shovel to the backing picture with a blob of silicone at the top and at the bottom.

3 Attach the rabbits, using blobs of silicone on the end of a toothpick at 1 cm/½ in intervals as the piece is quite long. Attach the bread and tray.

4 Fold the front table leg lengthwise to shape it, then attach it with silicone. Attach the other table leg.

Sheet 4

1 Cut out the four rabbits in one piece, leaving off the legs of the bench, the feet and the right arm of the mother rabbit and the feet of the baker bunny. Cut out the bread without the tray. Colour the cut edges as before.

2 Shape the bread so it sits slightly forward, then attach it with silicone.

3 Attach the rabbits with blobs of silicone placed at 1 cm/½ in intervals across the piece.

Sheet 5

1 Cut out the baker's hat and the rabbit's ear. Cut out and colour the edges of the cuffs of the baker's pants. Cut out the tin on the left, the bread dough, the head, ribbon, cape and arm of the mother rabbit, the small rabbit in the red beret without the feet and tail, the cooked bread, the assistant baker without the tail and the arm holding the tray, the baker's sleeve, the baker's shirt, the baker's pants. Colour all the edges and shape.

2 Attach all the pieces with appropriate numbers of silicone blobs.

Sheet 6

1 Cut out the baker's head, the small rabbit's head and arm and left front of pants, the assistant's yellow cuff, the green bow tie and the arm and sleeve holding the cake tray,

the two rows of cakes on the tray, the baker's apron and ties, the baker's tail. Colour all the edges and shape.

2 Attach all the pieces with appropriate numbers of silicone blobs.

Finishing

Coating the assembled picture with a gloss is optional, but as the aim is to make the finished paper look like tin, I always add varnish.

1 Load the brush with a small amount of the hi-gloss thinner, then load the brush with the varnish. The thinner allows the varnish to go on more evenly. Apply two coats, allowing the varnish to dry between coats.

2 Have your picture framed professionally with a suitably coloured mat and the little verse underneath.

Sheet 1

Sheet 2

Sheet 3

Sheet 4

Sheet 5

Sheet 6

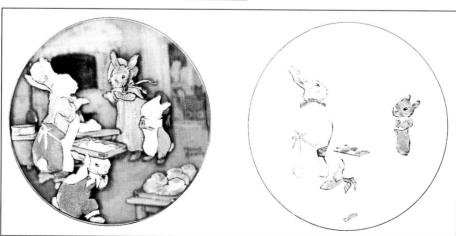

SILK RIBBON EMBROIDERY

Beautiful flowers and silk ribbons just seem to belong together. These days, the range of colours available in three widths of silk ribbons make it possible for the embroiderer to create an absolute cornucopia of flowers.

Embroidering with silk ribbon is suitable for the beginner and the expert stitcher alike. The stitches used are basically the same as those used in more traditional embroidery, with the addition of ribbon stitch (which is described in the Embroidery Guide, beginning on page 184) and some variations in technique. The softness of the ribbon ensures that it shapes easily to the stitch you are forming and lies well on the fabric.

Silk ribbon embroidery can produce large dramatic pieces, such as the Flower Basket Picture on page 76, or delicate tiny pieces, such as the Embroidered Brooch on page 80, or the Monogrammed Pillow on page 88.

Pillows are a particularly pretty way to show off silk ribbon embroidery and there are several examples in this chapter. On page 78, heart-shaped garlands of flowers and a smiling cherub adorn two damask pillows. Pansies are a perennial favourite, but are not often seen in silk embroidery. On page 85, silk ribbon pansies have been worked over lace to create a tiny silk pillow that is truly unique.

The effect of silk ribbon embroidery need not be delicate – it can be quite country and robust. The picture on page 83 is a perfect example of this, as is the wall hanging of embroidered country houses on page 91.

Flower Basket Picture

STITCHED BY BEVERLY SHELDRICK

This charming picture uses the same silk ribbon embroidery techniques as are used on small cushions and the like. The difference is that here they are bold in size, making a terrific impact.

Materials

- ❧ 45 cm/18 in square of linen
- ❧ 30 cm/12 in embroidery hoop
- ❧ an assortment of Piecemaker tapestry needles, sizes 20 to 24
- ❧ silk ribbon in a variety of widths and colours
- ❧ silk embroidery thread in colours to match the ribbon and the basket
- ❧ two gold cherubs
- ❧ sewing thread
- ❧ fine water-soluble marker pen
- ❧ craft glue

Method

See the Basket and Handle Patterns on Pull Out Pattern Sheet 1.

Preparation

Using the marker pen, lightly draw in the basket and handle shape on the linen or baste them in with sewing thread. Note that the base of the basket is 7.5 cm/3 in wide and the basket is 5 cm/2 in high. The handle is 16 cm/6½ in high and approximately 11 cm/4½ in wide at its widest point.

Embroidery

For the basket

1 Stitch the basketweave, using 4 mm/³⁄₁₆ in wide silk ribbon, held in place with tiny French knots in matching silk thread at the intersections of the weaving. The base of the basket is couched over the weaving with a contrasting 7 mm/⁵⁄₁₆ in wide silk ribbon.

2 The handle is worked in straight stitches of 7 mm/⁵⁄₁₆ in wide silk ribbon in the same colour as the basket, couched over with the same ribbon as the basket base.

For the flowers

Embroider the flowers in a variety of stitches and colours to please yourself, using the stitches described on pages 184-187. Use the picture as a guide, if you wish to have something similar, or be daring and design your own.

To finish off

1 Tie a bow in a 130 cm/52 in length of 7 mm/³⁄₁₆ in wide silk ribbon. Attach the bow and tails over the handle of the basket, using tiny French knots in matching silk embroidery thread to keep the graceful shape of the bow and the bow tails.

2 Glue on the two cherubs, entwining their arms in the ribbon tails.

Embroidered Pillows

MADE BY GLORIA MCKINNON

A heart-shaped garland of silk ribbon flowers is the perfect foil for a ruffled cushion. For a dramatic effect, embroider it on a black linen cushion and embellish it with a cherub. The same embroidery creates a totally different effect on a rich gold brocade cushion or framed as a picture.

Materials

For each cushion:

- ♣ 60 cm/24 in of 150 cm/60 in wide fabric
- ♣ silk ribbon in various colours and widths
- ♣ matching sewing thread
- ♣ an assortment of Piecemaker tapestry needles, sizes 20 and 22, and crewel needles, size 8
- ♣ tailors chalk
- ♣ tracing paper and pencil
- ♣ 24 cm/9 ½ in cushion insert or polyester fibre fill
- ♣ bread dough or sculptured cherub

Method

See the Embroidery Guide and the Heart Pattern on Pull Out Pattern Sheet 1.

Embroidery

1 Cut two 20 cm/8 in squares from the fabric for the cushion front and back.

2 Fold one square of linen into quarters and mark the centre. Trace the heart pattern, cut it out and draw the outline centred over the middle point. Baste around the shape of the heart.

3 Embroider the flowers around the heart, using the stitches and ribbon indicated in the stitch guide and on pages 184-187. When the embroidery is complete, glue on the cherub.

Assembling

1 Cut two strips 20 cm x 150 cm/8 in x 60 in for the ruffle. Sew the ends together to form a circle. Fold the ruffle strip over double with wrong sides together and raw edges even. Divide the length of the ruffle into quarters and mark them with pins.

2 Gather up the ruffle and pin it to the right side of the embroidered linen with raw edges even and the pins placed at the corners. Adjust the gathering. Baste then stitch the ruffle into place.

3 Fold the ruffle over on to the embroidered fabric. Place the cushion front and back pieces together with right sides facing. Stitch around the outside edge in the stitching line of the ruffle, leaving an opening on one side for turning. Turn the cushion through to the right side.

4 Place the insert inside the cover or stuff the cover quite firmly with the fibre fill, then slipstitch the opening closed.

If you are making the embroidered picture, embroider a square of fabric in the same way as for the cushion. Press around the embroidery so as not to flatten it, before framing it yourself or having it framed professionally.

Embroidered Brooch

STITCHED BY GLORIA MCKINNON

This delicate brooch or pendant, embroidered with a spray of silk ribbon flowers, would be a gift for someone very special to treasure. Make several in different colour combinations or flower shapes.

Materials

- ❧ 15 cm (6 in) square of linen
- ❧ brooch frame and back
- ❧ sharp pencil
- ❧ 10 cm (4 in) embroidery hoop
- ❧ 2 mm (¹⁄₁₆ in) of wide silk ribbon in the following colours and quantities: 1.5 m (1²⁄₃ yd) Dark Pink, 3 m (3¹⁄₃ yd) Medium Pink, 3 m (3¹⁄₃ yd) Light Pink, 2 m (2¹⁄₄ yd) Green, 1 m (1¹⁄₄ yd) Cream
- ❧ 1 m (1¹⁄₄ yd) Gold thread
- ❧ silk buttonhole twist, Green
- ❧ an assortment of Piecemaker needles, sizes 24 to 26

Method

1 On the square of linen, draw around the inner circumference of the brooch frame with the pencil. Place the fabric in the embroidery hoop and make it taut.

2 Using the Green silk buttonhole twist, stitch seven long straight stitches and then seven slightly shorter ones at the bottom to form the stems (Fig. 1).

3 Using the three shades of Pink silk ribbon and following the stitch guide on pages 184-187, embroider a rose at the top of each stem. Begin by making a colonial or French knot in the centre, using the Dark Pink. Surround the centre with four straight stitches in the Medium Pink, overlapping them for approximately one-third of their length. Try to 'snuggle' each stitch in close to the preceding one (Fig. 2).

4 At this point the rose will appear quite square. To soften this outline, work six or seven straight stitches in the Light Pink, overlapping them as before (Fig. 3).

5 To complete the bouquet, add a few buds by making a small ribbon stitch in Dark Pink and surrounding it with an open fly stitch in Green silk. The baby's breath is worked in scattered French knots in Cream silk ribbon.

6 For the leaves, stitch fly stitch greenery in Green silk ribbon. Finally, work a bow in the Gold thread around the waist of the bouquet by making a loop on one side and couching it in two places. Make a matching loop on the other side. Close the centre with a straight stitch. The bow tails are straight stitch with a couple of small straight stitches worked at right angles to the tails.

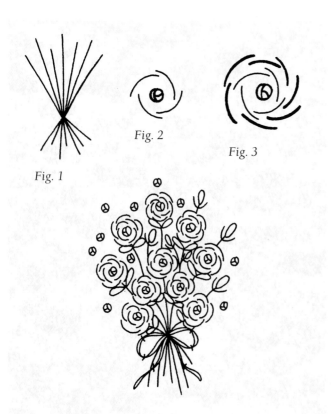

Fig. 1

Fig. 2

Fig. 3

Yesterday and Today

EMBROIDERED BY LYN SYLVESTER

This delightful picture of silk-embroidered flowers was inspired by the old tea cosy. The tea cosy was embroidered in stranded cotton which gives it a country cottage feel. For the picture, the same design has been interpreted in silk threads and ribbons.

Materials

- ❧ 46 cm x 36 cm (18 in x 14 in) of cream linen
- ❧ one pack each of Madeira silk thread, Dark Brown, Light Brown, Grass Green
- ❧ one card each of Kanagawa silk thread, Light Brown, Blue/Green, Light Olive, Olive
- ❧ one hank of Marlitt silk thread, Butter Yellow
- ❧ one hank each of Rajmahal silk thread, Yellow, Black
- ❧ 3.5 m (3¾ yd) of 4 mm (³⁄₁₆ in) wide silk ribbon, Medium Blue
- ❧ 3 m (3¼ yd) of 4 mm (³⁄₁₆ in) wide silk ribbon, Dark Blue
- ❧ 2 m (2¼ yd) of 4 mm (³⁄₁₆ in) wide silk ribbon, Purple
- ❧ 4.5 m (5 yd) of 4 mm (³⁄₁₆ in) wide silk ribbon, Gold
- ❧ 2.5 m (2¾ yd) of 3 mm (⅛ in) wide silk ribbon, Dark Coral Pink, Medium Pink
- ❧ 1.5 m (1⅔ yd) of 3 mm (⅛ in) wide silk ribbon, Light Pink
- ❧ 1.5 m (1⅔ yd) of 4 mm (³⁄₁₆ in) wide silk ribbon, Light Blue
- ❧ 1.5 m (1⅔ yd) of 4 mm (³⁄₁₆ in) wide silk ribbon, Butter Yellow
- ❧ 1 m (1⅛ yd) of 2 mm (¹⁄₁₆ in) wide silk ribbon, Dusky Pink
- ❧ 1.3 m (1⅓ yd) of 7 mm (⁵⁄₁₆ in) wide silk ribbon, Bright Coral
- ❧ 50 cm (20 in) of 7 mm (⁵⁄₁₆ in) wide silk ribbon, Pale Coral
- ❧ 50 cm (20 in) of 7 mm (⁵⁄₁₆ in) wide silk ribbon, White
- ❧ 2 m (2¼ yd) of 4 mm (³⁄₁₆ in) wide silk ribbon, White

- ❧ 1 m (1⅛ yd) each of 7 mm (⁵⁄₁₆ in) wide silk ribbon, Lavender, Mauve
- ❧ 50 cm (20 in) of 7 mm (⁵⁄₁₆ in) wide silk organza ribbon, Purple
- ❧ 50 cm (20 in) of 7 mm (⁵⁄₁₆ in) wide satin ribbon, Dark Purple
- ❧ 6 m (6½ yd) of 2 mm (¹⁄₁₆ in) wide silk ribbon, Green
- ❧ 2 m (2¼ yd) of 4 mm (³⁄₁₆ in) wide silk ribbon, Yellow/Green
- ❧ 1 m (1⅛ yd) of 4 mm (³⁄₁₆ in) wide silk ribbon, Green
- ❧ an assortment of Piecemaker tapestry needles, sizes 20 to 24
- ❧ pencil or fine water-soluble marker pen

Method

See the Embroidery Guide on Pull Out Pattern Sheet 2.

1 On the piece of linen and using the pencil or the marker pen, draw in the position of major elements of the design such as the fence.

2 Embroider the design, following the stitch guide on pages 184-187 and using the stitches and threads indicated on page 84.

3 When the embroidery is completed, have it framed professionally if you are not able to frame it yourself. Take care to choose a coloured mat that complements the colours of the embroidery without overwhelming it.

Stitch Guide

1 Back fence, ground and path markings: stem stitch and straight stitch in two strands of Dark Brown Madeira thread

2 Stone wall: stem stitch in Light Brown Kanagawa thread

3 Crazy paving wall: stem stitch in two strands of Light Brown Madeira thread

4 Grass clumps: stem stitch and straight stitch in two strands of Grass Green Madeira thread

5 Daffodils: lazy daisy stitch in Gold silk ribbon; the throat is three buttonhole stitches in Yellow Rajmahal thread

6 Blue crocus: lazy daisy stitch in Light Blue and Dark Blue silk ribbon; the centre is bullion stitch in one strand of Marlitt Butter Yellow thread

7 Small blue flowers: straight stitch in Light Blue, Medium Blue and Dark Blue silk ribbon; the centre is a four-strand French knot in Black Rajmahal thread

8 Small pink flowers: straight stitch in Light Pink, Medium Pink and Dark Coral Pink silk ribbon, the centre is a French knot in Dusky Pink silk ribbon

9 Buttercups: lazy daisy stitch in Butter Yellow silk ribbon, the centre is a French knot in Gold silk ribbon

10 White crocus: lazy daisy stitch in 4 mm (³⁄16 in) wide White silk ribbon, the centre is a bullion stitch in one strand of Marlitt Butter Yellow thread

11 Violets: lazy daisy stitch in Purple silk ribbon, the centre is a Gold silk ribbon French knot

12 Tulips: ribbon stitch in Bright Coral silk ribbon

13 Tulips: ribbon stitch in a mix of Bright Coral, Pale Coral and 7 mm (⁵⁄16 in) wide White silk ribbon

14 Tulips: ribbon stitch in Purple organza ribbon and Dark Purple satin ribbon

15 Tulips: ribbon stitch in Lavender and Mauve silk ribbon

16 Daisies: lazy daisy stitch in 4 mm (³⁄16 in) White silk ribbon, the centre is a Gold silk ribbon French knot

17 Crocus leaves: straight stitch in Grass Green Madeira thread

18 Daisy stems: stem stitch in Green silk ribbon

19 Tulip leaves: twisted ribbon stitch in Yellow/Green silk ribbon

20 Tulip stems: stem stitch in Olive Kanagawa thread

21 Small pink and blue flower stems: whipped chain stitch (see note) in Blue/Green Kanagawa thread

22 Daffodil stems: double stem stitch in Blue/Green Kanagawa thread

23 Violet and buttercup leaves: lazy daisy stitch in Green silk ribbon

Note: Whipped chain stitch creates a wonderful knobbly stem. Work a row of simple chain stitches, then whip stitch over each chain.

Pansy Pillow

STITCHED BY GLORIA McKINNON

This charming little pillow combines delicate lace and silk ribbon embroidery to produce a unique effect. The pansies are slightly tricky to perfect, so take a little time to practise before you begin working on the lace.

Materials

- ♣ two pieces of moiré fabric, each 25 cm x 30 cm (10 in x 12 in)
- ♣ two 20 cm (8 in) wide strips of moiré fabric, cut across the full width of the fabric, for the ruffle
- ♣ 30 cm (12 in) of 12 cm (4^1/$_2$ in) wide lace
- ♣ 4 m (4^1/$_2$ yd) each of 4 mm (^{3}/$_{16}$ in) wide silk ribbon: Lemon Yellow, Blue/green, Pale Blue, Olive Green
- ♣ 2 m (2^1/$_4$ yd) each of 7 mm (^{5}/$_{16}$ in) wide silk ribbon: Purple, Violet
- ♣ 2 m (2^1/$_4$ yd) each of 4 mm (^{3}/$_{16}$ in) wide silk ribbon: Yellow, Black, Pink
- ♣ one card of Kanagawa silk thread, Olive Green
- ♣ one hank of embroidery thread, Blue/green
- ♣ 10 m (11 yd) of 4 mm (^{3}/$_{16}$ in) wide Pale Pink silk ribbon
- ♣ an assortment of Piecemaker tapestry needles, sizes 20 to 24
- ♣ 1 m (1^1/$_8$ yd) of piping cord
- ♣ 2.5 cm x 1 m (1 in x 1^1/$_8$ yd) of fabric for the piping
- ♣ matching sewing thread
- ♣ polyester fibre fill

Method

See the Embroidery Design and Key on Pull Out Pattern Sheet 3.

1 Baste the lace across the centre of one piece of the moiré fabric, matching centre lines.

2 Following the embroidery design and the stitch guide on page 86, embroider the pansies and other flowers as shown, taking the stitches through the lace and the moiré fabric. This is a little harder than the usual silk ribbon embroidery, but persevere – it will be worth it.

For the piping

1 Fold the piping fabric over double with the wrong sides together. Place the piping cord inside the folded fabric.

Using the zipper foot on your sewing machine, stitch along the length of the piping, as close as possible to the cord.

2 Pin the piping around the right side of the embroidered piece with the raw edges even and the piping towards the centre of the fabric. Clip the seam allowance of the piping to allow it to curve around the corners, overlapping the ends.

3 Trim the ends of the piping so that one end overlaps the other end for 2.5 cm (1 in). Undo the stitching for 2.5 cm (1 in) on the longer end and cut out the cord for this length. Turn a small hem on the longer end of the fabric. Lay the shorter end of the piping inside the hemmed end. Using the zipper foot on your sewing machine, stitch around the pillow to secure the piping, stitching as close to the cord as you can.

For the ruffle

1 Join the two strips of fabric together to form a circle. Fold the circle over double with the wrong sides together and the raw edges even. Divide the length of the circle into quarters and mark these points with pins.

2 Sew two rows of gathering stitches along the raw edge of the ruffle. Pull up the gathering to fit around the pillow. Pin the ruffle to the right side of the pillow front, placing a pin at each corner. Adjust the gathering, then stitch on the wrong side following the piping stitching line.

Assembling

1 Place the pillow front on top of the pillow back with the ruffle pointing towards the centre of the pillow. Stitch around three sides and for 2.5 cm (1 in) on both ends of the fourth side, stitching along the same line as before.

2 Clip across the corners and turn the pillow to the right side. Carefully stuff the pillow, taking care to push the stuffing into the corners. Slipstitch the opening closed.

Stitch Guide

Pansy

Using straight stitches and the 7 mm (⁵/₁₆ in) wide Violet or Purple silk ribbon, work six straight stitches from the centre outwards (Fig. 1). Take care to place stitch number 6 slightly over stitches 4 and 5 (Fig. 2).

Using the 4 mm (³/₁₆ in) wide Black silk ribbon, work four straight stitches over the top of the first stitches (Fig. 3). Make a Yellow French knot in the centre.

Jenny Bradford's Wrapped Rose

These roses are worked in three shades of 4 mm (³/₁₆ in) wide silk ribbon.

Work a French knot in the darkest shade for the centre.

Work three curved whipped stitches around the centre in the medium colour (Fig. 4). To work a whipped stitch, make a straight stitch, then whip the ribbon over it three or four times (Fig. 5). With the last of these, pass the thread through to the back.

Work another row of five whipped stitches around the centre in the lightest shade (Fig. 6).

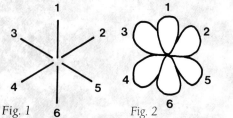

Fig. 1   Fig. 2

Fig. 3

Fig. 4

Fig. 5

Fig. 6

Monogrammed Pillow

Stitched by Gloria McKinnon

Pretty pillows are a great way to dress up a room.

Materials

- ❧ 90 cm (36 in) of moiré fabric
- ❧ one Swiss-embroidered initial motif
- ❧ 5 m (5¹/₂ yd) of 3 mm (³/₁₆ in) wide silk ribbon, Pale Pink, Yellow
- ❧ 2 m (2¹/₄ yd) of 7 mm (⁵/₁₆ in) wide silk ribbon, Pale Blue
- ❧ 2 m (2¹/₄ yd) of 3 mm (³/₁₆ in) wide silk ribbon, Lilac
- ❧ DMC Stranded Cotton, Green 523, Ecru
- ❧ cherub
- ❧ machine-sewing thread to match the fabric
- ❧ Piecemaker tapestry needle, size 22
- ❧ crewel embroidery needle, size 8
- ❧ 18 cm (7 in) cushion insert
- ❧ craft glue

Method

Use 6 mm (¹/₄ in) seams throughout.

1 Cut two 18 cm (7 in) squares from the moiré fabric. Baste the initial motif to the centre of one of the squares.

2 Embroider the floral garland around the initial motif, following the embroidery design and key below. Take the embroidery over the edges of the motif, concealing the edges. Make sure you leave sufficient space at the top for the cherub.

3 Cut three 24 cm (9¹/₂ in) wide strips across the width of the fabric for the ruffle. Join the three strips together to make a loop. Fold the loop over double with the wrong sides together and the raw edges even. Divide the length of the loop into quarters and mark the quarter points with a pin.

4 Gather the raw edges. Pin the ruffle around the right side of the embroidered piece with the raw edges even, the quarter points at the corners and the frill lying towards the centre. Adjust the gathering, then stitch on the ruffle.

5 Place the front and back together with the right sides facing. Stitch around in the ruffle stitching line, leaving 12 cm (4³/₄ in) open on one side. Trim the corners, then turn the pillow cover to the right side. Push out the corners carefully. Place the insert inside the cover. Slipstitch the opening closed. Glue on the cherub.

Ribbon roses in straight stitch with three French knots in the centre

Leaves in detached chain stitch in one strand of green

Daisies in ribbon stitch with a yellow French knot in the centre

Baby's breath in French knots in one strand of ecru

Wisteria in French knots of lilac silk ribbon

Rosebuds in pale pink ribbon stitch with calyx and stem in straight stitch in one strand of green

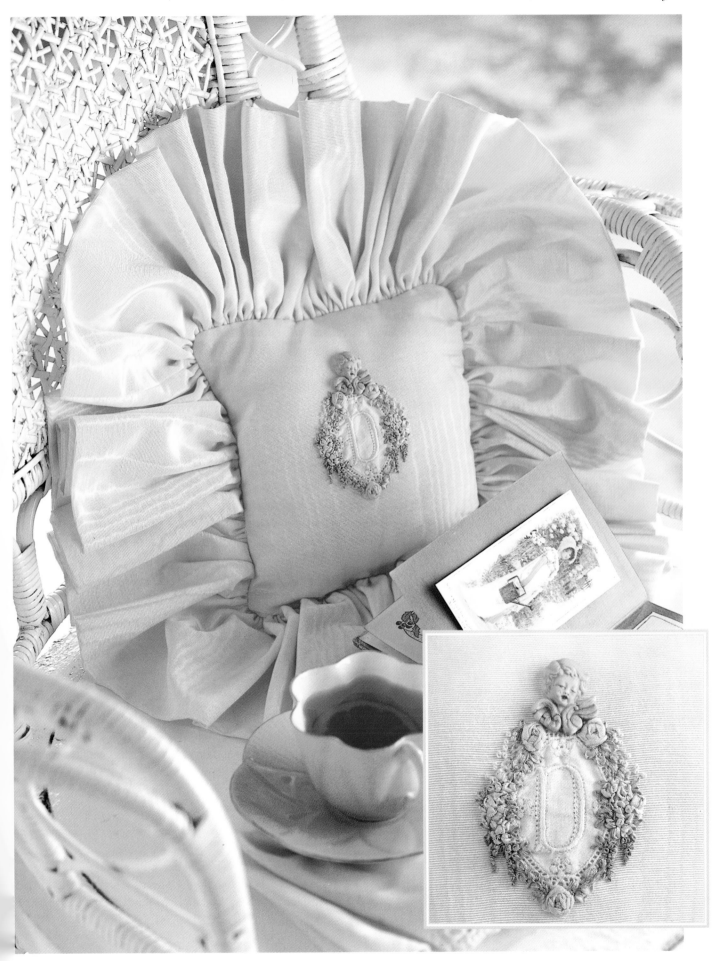

Embroidered Wallhanging

STITCHED BY GLORIA McKINNON

Simple pre-printed panels are brought to life, embellished with silk ribbon embroidery and paint. If you just want to paint a simple picture and embroider it, we have included a single house on the pattern sheet for you to trace and embroider.

Finished size: 68 cm x 78 cm (27 in x 31 in)

Materials

- ♣ set of six pre-printed houses (on linen) or a piece of linen 19 cm x 25 cm (7½ in x 10 in) for the single house
- ♣ Jo Sonja Colors: Blue, Green, Terracotta, Cream
- ♣ paintbrush
- ♣ silk ribbons in a variety of colours for the embroidery
- ♣ 20 cm (8 in) of two fabrics for the sashing and borders
- ♣ 50 cm (20 in) of main fabric
- ♣ 20 cm (8 in) of binding fabric
- ♣ 75 cm (30 in) of backing fabric
- ♣ 75 cm (30 in) of wadding
- ♣ quilting thread
- ♣ quilting needles
- ♣ Pigma pen, sepia
- ♣ masking tape for the single house
- ♣ length of dowel

Method

Embroidery

For the pre-printed panels

1 Make a very light wash with the paints and lightly touch up the backgrounds of the sky, grass and houses. Allow the paint to dry.

2 Embroider the houses using straight stitches, French knots and lazy daisy stitch, following the stitch guide on pages 184-187. Work the leaves and flowers in ribbon stitch.

For the single house

See the Design on Pull Out Pattern Sheet 3.

Trace the design from the pattern sheet directly onto the 19 cm x 25 cm (7½ in x 10 in) piece of linen with the Pigma pen. It is quite simple to do this by taping the design to a window with the linen taped over the top. Colour the house and background with light paint washes, then embroider the picture as for the pieced panel.

Finishing

For the block borders

Cut border strips 3 cm (1¼ in) wide. Sew a border strip to the top and bottom of each block, trim the length even with the block edge, then sew the border to the side edges.

For the sashing

1 Cut the sashing strips 6.5 cm (2½ in) wide. Join two panels with a length of the sashing in between, using 6 mm (¼ in) seam allowances. Repeat this for the other two pairs.

2 Join together the three rows made in step 1 with a length of sashing in between.

3 For the outer border, measure the length of the pieced panel, then cut four 11 cm (4½ in) wide strips of the main fabric to this length. Sew the border on the top and bottom first, then on the sides.

4 Place the backing face down with the wadding on top and the pieced panel on top of that. Baste the three layers together, stitching through the centre vertically, horizontally, diagonally and around the edges. Outline-quilt around each block and around the borders.

5 Fold the 5 cm (2 in) wide strip of binding fabric in half, lengthwise, with the wrong sides together. Press. Pin the binding to the top and bottom of the panel with the raw edges even, stitch, then attach the binding to the sides in the same way. Turn the binding to the back of the quilt and slipstitch it into place.

6 For the casing, cut a 10 cm (4 in) wide strip of fabric 62 cm (24½ in) long from the backing fabric. Fold it in half, lengthwise, and turn in 6 mm (¼ in) on the raw edges at each end. Fold under the remaining raw edges. Press, then slipstitch it onto the backing, near the top. Pass the length of dowel through the casing for hanging.

FLOWER CRAFTS

Flowers have probably been used as decorations for thousands of years. Freshly-picked blooms bring the pleasures of the garden indoors for us to enjoy as we go about our day. The absence of fresh flowers does not mean we need to forego this simple pleasure. Today, dried flowers or flowers made from silk or other fabrics, paper or lifelike man-made materials are readily available. The challenge comes in choosing the style of the composition and suitable containers or trimmings to complement that style.

The Floral Foursome on page 94 is an example of a very simple concept, using terracotta pots and a variety of dried flowers to create a country look. A very different effect is achieved with similar materials in the little framed topiary on page 103.

Flowers and romance have always been associated and the lovely Romantic Swag on page 96 shows us why. Tiny pink flowers and leaves are complemented by the dramatic touches of gold, echoed in those guardians of romance – the two cherubs who support the swag.

Christmas is the time we all associate with pine cones and berries. On page 98, there is a traditional Christmas wreath to make for the front door.

Flowers can turn a utilitarian item into an object of beauty, still useful, but decorative at the same time. On page 100, simple baskets have been transformed with spray paint and full-blown roses.

Floral Foursome

MADE BY GLORIA McKINNON

Terracotta and pine give a warm 'country' feel to this dried flower wall picture which would look great in a sunny kitchen or family room.

Materials

- ♣ 40 cm x 70 cm/16 in x 28 in pine backboard or ten 7 cm wide x 40 cm long /3 in wide x 16 in long tongue and groove boards to make your own backboard
- ♣ four lengths of mitred pine, two pieces 7 cm x 40 cm/3 in x 16 in and two pieces 7 cm x 70 cm/3 in x 28 in, for the frame
- ♣ two 10 cm/4 in terracotta pots or four half terracotta pots
- ♣ small block of oasis
- ♣ dried flowers, such as lavender, roses, daisies, larkspur
- ♣ 75 cm/30 in wired ribbon
- ♣ 3 m/3¼ yd raffia
- ♣ small amount of moss
- ♣ wood glue or hammer and nails
- ♣ wire and ring hooks for hanging
- ♣ hot melt glue gun

Method

1 If you are making your own backboard, glue or nail the tongue and groove boards together.

2 Nail or glue the lengths of mitred pine together to form a frame. Nail or glue the frame to the backboard.

3 If you are using the 10 cm/4 in terracotta pots, cut them in half. Using the glue gun, glue the half pots in a straight line across the backboard at the marked points. Place the pots so that they appear to be resting on the top edge of the bottom of the frame. Glue a small piece of oasis into each of the pots.

4 Push the flower stems into the oasis, taking care to keep them straight. When all the flowers are in place, glue a little moss around the base of the flowers, covering the oasis.

5 Tie bows from the ribbon and from the raffia and glue them to the front of the pots.

Romantic Swag

MADE BY NOLA MCCARTHY

A graceful swag makes a wonderful wall decoration.

Materials

- ❧ plaited raffia swag, approximately 110 cm (43 in) long
- ❧ two 2.5 cm (1 in) brass rings
- ❧ darning or carpet needle
- ❧ strong thread
- ❧ six bunches of large berries or crab apples
- ❧ ten spikes of holly berries and leaves
- ❧ eight sprays of dusty pink small roses
- ❧ twelve sprays of small dusty pink flowers
- ❧ twenty-four sprays of blackberries and leaves
- ❧ two gold plaster cherubs
- ❧ paint, Gold
- ❧ paintbrush
- ❧ glue gun

Method

1 Using the thread doubled and the darning or carpet needle, sew the brass rings to the back of the swag where the ends are tied.

2 Paint all the holly leaves and berries with the Gold paint. Set them aside to dry. Dab Gold paint at random on to the blackberry leaves. Set them aside to dry. Paint the edges of some of the rose petals with the Gold paint. Set them aside to dry.

3 Working from the ends into the centre and using the glue gun, first attach the large gold berries and leaves to provide a base for the other flowers. At the centre of the swag, increase the width by adding extra berries and leaves, twisting the stems together for added strength.

4 Attach the smaller holly berries and leaves, placing them around the edge. Glue on the roses, making sure that no stems are visible. Pull the berries forward a little so they nestle among the roses, not behind them. Glue on the small flowers around and between the roses. Finally, push all the blackberry spikes in amongst the flowers, positioning some at the edges to add to the width and define the curved shape of the swag. Add some more blackberry spikes among the flowers to balance out the colours. Attach the cherubs to the wall, then support the swag between them.

GILDED CHERUB FROM PARTERRE GARDEN, WOOLLAHRA, NSW

Christmas Wreath

Made by Nola McCarthy

So easy to make, this simple wreath on your front door will offer a warm welcome to Christmas visitors.

Materials

- ❦ 300 mm x 580 mm (11³/₄ in x 22³/₄ in) rough sawn board
- ❦ acrylic paint: Green, Gold
- ❦ 25 cm (10 in) diameter wreath
- ❦ twelve to fifteen green Christmas spikes with berries
- ❦ twelve small pine cones
- ❦ glue gun
- ❦ 90 cm (36 in) of 10 cm (4 in) wide paper ribbon
- ❦ foam brush

Method

1 Paint the board with the Green paint. This does not need to be a completely smooth even paint cover. Allow the paint to dry.

2 With the Gold paint, paint a 2.5 cm (1 in) wide border around the board. Allow the paint to dry.

3 Using the glue gun, attach the wreath securely to the centre of the board.

4 Beginning at the top of the wreath, glue on the Christmas spikes. Makes sure each spike covers the stem of the previously attached spike and that some of the spikes protrude over the edges of the wreath. Glue on the pine cones.

5 Lightly dab the berries and cones with Gold paint to create highlights.

6 Tie a large bow with the ribbon and glue it into position at the bottom of the wreath. Dab a little Gold paint on the bow as well.

Rose Basket

DECORATED BY NOLA MCCARTHY

A decorated basket is useful as well as decorative – a great way to store sewing needs, knitting wool, soaps and towels or just about anything you can think of. Following these simple instructions, you can trim a basket of any shape or size.

Materials

- ❧ basket
- ❧ acrylic paint, Green, Gold
- ❧ paintbrushes
- ❧ three sprays of rosehips and leaves
- ❧ one paper rose with a bud (you can use a silk rose, if you wish)
- ❧ 150 cm (59 in) of 15 cm (6 in) wide green/mauve Sinnamay ribbon
- ❧ two lengths of florists wire or another light gauge wire
- ❧ craft glue or a glue gun

Method

1 Paint the basket inside and out with the green paint, then set it aside to dry.

2 Gently twist the mesh ribbon to give it a corded look. Measure around the basket where you wish the ribbon to sit. If your basket has two handles on the side, you can measure from handle to handle. Twist a length of the florists wire around the ribbon at that length.

3 If your basket has a handle on the side, cut the ribbon 2.5 cm (1 in) beyond the wire tie. If there are two handles, treat both ends in the same way so that you will actually have two lengths of ribbon. Thread the ends of the wire or wires through the basket to secure the ends of the ribbon, then glue the ribbon to the basket. If your basket has no handles, allow the ends of the ribbon to cross over, secure them with the wire, then pass the wire through the basket to secure it. Glue the ribbon to the basket. Open out the ends of the ribbon.

4 Using the Gold paint, lightly daub around the basket rim and the base. If there are handles, dab a little Gold paint on them as well. Lightly dab a little Gold paint on the roses and rosehips. With just the tiniest drop of paint on your brush, touch the mesh ribbon very lightly. Allow all the paint to dry before you go any further.

5 Arrange the flowers and leaves over the ends of the ribbon. You can use the same placement as shown here or use an arrangement of your own. Glue the flowers and leaves in place, using the craft glue or the glue gun. Be generous with the glue to ensure that all the trimmings are securely attached.

Silk-lined Basket

LINED BY MARG MANNING

A basket of any shape and size can be lined with fabric. Simply measure the height and circumference of your own basket to calculate how much fabric you will need.

Materials

- ❧ two pieces of fabric: one that is as long as twice the circumference of the basket and as wide as the depth of the basket plus 10 cm (4 in), and another that is the size of the base of the basket plus 5 cm (2 in) all around
- ❧ a piece of Pellon fleece, the same size as the base of the basket
- ❧ fabric for the piping, 2.5 cm (1 in) wide
- ❧ firm cord for the piping
- ❧ cardboard
- ❧ spray adhesive
- ❧ sewing thread
- ❧ hand-sewing needle
- ❧ craft glue or a glue gun

Method

1 Using the cardboard, make a template of the inside base of the basket. Using the template, cut the Pellon to the same shape. Spray one side of the cardboard with the adhesive and attach the Pellon to it.

2 Baste around the edge of the fabric piece for the base. Place the Pellon-covered cardboard on the wrong side of the fabric with the Pellon side closest to the fabric. Draw up the basting so that the fabric pulls firmly over the cardboard. Tie off the thread to secure the gathering. Adjust the gathering and smooth the edges, then set the piece aside.

3 Fold the fabric for the piping over the piping cord with the wrong sides together. Using the zipper foot on your sewing machine stitch as close to the cord as you can.

4 Join the short ends of the rectangular fabric piece. Sew two rows of gathering around the top edge, then pull up the gathering to fit the lip of the basket, then secure the ends of the thread. Adjust the gathers so that they are even.

5 Pin the piping to the right side of the gathered fabric with the raw edges even, but do not cut off any excess piping.

6 Cut the piping 2.5 cm (1 in) longer than you actually need so that one end overlaps the other end for 2.5 cm (1 in). Undo the stitching on the overlapping part of the piping and cut the cord out of that section so that the two

ends of the cord meet exactly. Turn a small hem on the overlapping fabric and tuck the other end of the piping inside it. This makes a very neat join on the piping.

7 Stitch the piping to the gathered fabric, using a regular stitch length and the zipper foot on your sewing machine and stitching as close as possible to the piping cord.

8 Fold the raw edge of the gathered fabric to the wrong side so that the piping sits up. Fit the fabric into the basket, then glue it into place at the top edge, taking care to keep the gathering even and the piping sitting up straight.

9 The remaining length of piping is attached to the base piece. You may need to clip the seam allowance of the piping to enable it to curve to the shape of the base properly. Join the ends of the piping as for the top edge, then glue the piping to the wrong side of the base liner so that only the piping cord is visible from the right side.

10 Adjust the gathering at the bottom of the basket, then glue the base piece over the raw edge. Hold the base in place for a moment to ensure that it will stay in place

Lisel Heeps who made this charming topiary picture was first introduced to this technique by Kathleen Mathews, a dried flower artist. It is made in a very similar way to the one on page 94, except that you will need to create a base for the flower ball from twigs. When you have attached the half pot and trunk, glue four 7 cm/3 in twigs into an open square at the top of the trunk. Glue the dried flowers over this frame until you have a nice round shape.

SEWING AND EMBROIDERY

Ever since cave men stitched hides together with bone needles, people have sewed for utilitarian purposes. As social groups settled and began to cultivate the land, sewing took on an added decorative dimension. Through the ages, this dimension has blossomed into an art form until today, we have textile artists and embroiderers working exclusively with manipulated and embellished fabric.

Simple sewing and embroidery can work together to produce items of practicality and beauty, such as the Draught Stopper on page 106. Other utilitarian items can be transformed when they are constructed from beautiful fabric and lavishly trimmed. The Velvet-covered Coathanger on page 112 is certainly a far cry from the old wire coathanger that lurks in so many closets!

Smocking is another traditional craft, recorded as early as the fifteenth century. For centuries after, it was used to shape the simple smocks (hence the name) worn by country folk. These days, smocking is more likely to be used decoratively on children's clothes and sleepwear. On page 109, the Doll's Dress has been smocked to produce a charming Victorian image.

Rich and dramatic, crazy quilting has been around for many years. Usually made up of patches of rich fabrics, crazy quilt pieces are then lavishly embroidered, often with mottos or traditional motifs. The Crazy Quilt Purse on page 118, is so densely embroidered that it is sometimes difficult to see where the fabric peeps through.

One of the most pleasurable and satisfying forms of sewing is toymaking. Whether you are making a doll for a small girl or a teddy bear for a new baby, there is a great deal of joy in seeing the beams of pleasure your gift inspires. The cuddly Teddy Bear on page 125 is sure to delight someone you know.

Draught Stopper

Made by Fay King

Functional items can be beautiful! This draught stopper will keep the chilly winds of winter out of your home and add a charming touch at the same time.

Materials

- ❧ 18 cm x 91.5 cm (7 in x 36 in) of cotton velveteen
- ❧ tailors chalk
- ❧ tracing paper
- ❧ pencil
- ❧ DMC Stranded Cotton: 223 Dark Shell Pink,
  224 Medium Shell Pink, 225 Light Shell Pink,
  3042 Antique Violet, 800 Delft Blue, 745 Light Yellow,
  3362 Dark Pine Green, 3052 Medium Grey-green, Ecru
- ❧ 1 m (40 in) of 3 mm (⅛ in) wide silk ribbon
- ❧ packet of straw needles, sizes 3 to 8
- ❧ polyester fibre fill

Note: If you wish the draught stopper to be more weighty, you can use a mixture of sand and sawdust for the filling. Make sure the filling is thoroughly dry. If you do use sand and sawdust, it is a good idea to make a calico liner in the same size as the velvet piece. Slip the calico inside the velvet before adding the filling, securely close the calico liner, then close the velvet outer covering.

Method

See the Embroidery Design and the Scallop Template on Pull Out Pattern Sheet 2.

1 Using the tailors chalk, mark the centre line lengthwise and widthwise on the wrong side of the fabric. Measure 20 cm (8 in) on either side of the lengthwise centre line and mark these lines with the tailors chalk.

2 Trace the scallop template marking in the centre lines. Place the template on the wrong side of the fabric and, using the tailors chalk, draw in four scallops (Fig. 1). Baste in the scallop shape so that the stitches are clearly visible.

3 Embroider the scallops with garlands of flowers, following the embroidery design on the pattern sheet and the stitch guide given here. When the embroidery is completed, remove the basting threads.

4 Fold the fabric in half lengthwise, with the right sides together and the raw edges even. Join the long sides with a 1 cm (½ in) seam. Fold the fabric so that this seam lies across the centre back, then stitch one end closed.

5 Turn to the right side. Stuff firmly with the fibre fill. Turn in the raw fabric at the open end. Close the opening with ladder stitch, stitching loosely from side to side, then pulling up the thread firmly and securing it (Fig. 2).

Fig. 1

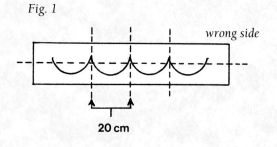

wrong side

20 cm

Fig. 2

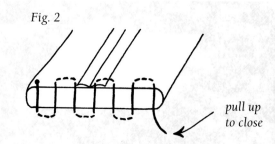

pull up to close

Draught Stopper Stitch Guide

All the roses, lavender and daisies are combinations of bullion stitches worked in appropriate colours. For the bullion stitch instructions, see the stitch guide on page 8.

Roses

Using six strands of DMC 223 and a size 3 straw needle, make three bullions side by side for the centre of the rose.

Using six strands of DMC 224, make five bullions, working clockwise around the centre and beginning each bullion inside the previous one.

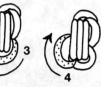

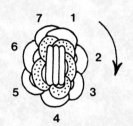
Using six strands of DMC 225 and a size 3 straw needle, make seven bullions, working clockwise around the centre, in the same way as those made in step 2.

Leaves

Using three strands of DMC 3362 and a size 6 straw needle, make a bullion from **a** to **b** with nine wraps. Ease them off the needle, then give the thread a tug which will tighten the wraps and taper the bullion. Take the needle to the back of your work at **c**.

Make a second bullion with eight wraps beside the first one and finish it in the same way.

Large rosebud

Using three strands of DMC 223 and a size 6 straw needle, make a satin stitch centre, stitching from **a** to **b** four times.

Using three strands of DMC 224 and a size 6 straw needle, make two bullions with ten wraps each on either side of the centre.

Using three strands of DMC 225 and a size 6 straw needle, make one bullion with twelve wraps on either side.

Using three strands of DMC 3362 and a size 6 straw needle, make one bullion with fourteen wraps on either side.

Small rosebud

Using three strands of DMC 223 and a size 6 straw needle, make one bullion with ten wraps, stitching from **a** to **b**.

Using three strands of DMC 224 and a size 6 straw needle, make one bullion with twelve wraps on either side of the centre.

Using three strands of DMC 3362 and a size 6 straw needle, make one bullion with fourteen wraps on either side. Tug the thread a little to taper the end. Work three tiny satin stitches across the bottom at **a**.

Lavender stems

Work the stems in stem stitch, using two strands of DMC 3052 and a size 8 straw needle.

Gloria's tip: To maintain a graceful curve with stem stitch, always keep the thread to the outside of the curve.

Lavender heads

Using three strands of DMC 3042 and a size 6 straw needle, make seven bullions of ten wraps each for each lavender head. Begin at the top of the stem, then work in the order indicated.

For the bow, bring narrow silk ribbon through from the back of the work and tie a bow at the front.

Daisies

Using two strands of DMC Ecru and a size 8 straw needle, make twelve bullions with ten wraps each, working from the centre outwards in

the order indicated in diagram on the previous page. Position the petals so that there is room for a yellow bullion with six wraps at the centre. Make the bud in the same way, following the diagram on the right.

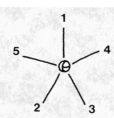

Forget-me-nots
Using three strands of DMC 800 and a size 6 straw needle, make five satin stitch petals in the order indicated on diagram on the left. For each petal, stitch three or four times from **a** to **b** as shown in the diagram on the right.

Make a French knot in the centre, using two strands of DMC 745 and a size 8 straw needle.

Doll's Dress

MADE BY ANNE'S GLORY BOX

Smocking is the ideal finish for this smart Victorian-style dress. Pick out the colours from the Liberty cotton print for the embroidery.

To fit: a 76 cm (30 in) doll

Materials

- ♣ 1.6 m (1³/₄ yd) of Liberty fabric
- ♣ 4 m (4¹/₂ yd) of 9 cm (3¹/₂ in) wide Swiss embroidery
- ♣ 60 cm (24 in) of 4 cm (1¹/₂ in) wide Swiss embroidery
- ♣ DMC Stranded Cotton: Burgundy, Green, Ecru
- ♣ 1.5 m (1²/₃ yd) of 3.5 cm (1³/₈ in) wide cream satin ribbon
- ♣ 1 m (1¹/₈ yd) of 6 mm (¹/₄ in) wide cream satin ribbon
- ♣ 1 m (1¹/₈ yd) of 6 mm (¹/₄ in) wide entredeux
- ♣ Piecemaker crewel needle, size 8
- ♣ press studs
- ♣ smocking pleater (optional)

Method

See the Pattern and the Smocking Plate on Pull Out Pattern Sheet 4.

For the smocking

1 Cut one piece of fabric for the front, 35 cm x 90 cm (13³/₄ in x 35¹/₂ in) and two pieces for the backs, each 35 cm x 45 cm (13³/₄ in x 17³/₄ in).

2 At the top edge of the front, draw up seven half-space rows with the smocking pleater, unless you prefer to use the smocking service provided by your local haberdashery store.

3 Undo the pleating for 1.5 cm (⁵/₈ in) from each edge and tie the threads off evenly in pairs.

4 Complete the smocking as shown on the smocking plate, then block the smocking to fit the front bodice.

For the bodice and sleeves

1 Join the front and back yokes at the shoulders, using a 6 mm (¹/₄ in) seam.

2 Cut a small piece of fabric, 5 cm x 35 cm (2 in x 13³/₄ in), on the bias. Press the piece over double with the wrong sides together.

3 Gather the narrow Swiss embroidery to fit the neck edge. Pin the gathered Swiss embroidery around the neck edge, both with right sides up. Adjust the gathering to ensure that it is even.

4 Pin the bias strip around the neck edge, over the Swiss embroidery, with all the raw edges even. Stitch. Turn the folded edge to the wrong side and slipstitch it into place, neatening the ends as you go.

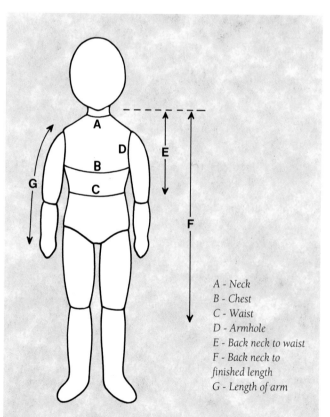

A - Neck
B - Chest
C - Waist
D - Armhole
E - Back neck to waist
F - Back neck to finished length
G - Length of arm

This dress has been made to fit a 76 cm (30 in) doll, but it is quite simple to adjust the pattern to suit a different-sized doll. Measure all the areas indicated in the diagram, then adjust the pattern accordingly. For awkward or very small measurements, use cotton tape or string to measure your doll, then check the length on a tape measure.

5 Sew entredeux around the sleeve ends. Gather the wide Swiss embroidery slightly and attach it to the entredeux.

6 Gather the sleeve heads as marked. Insert the sleeves into the armholes, pulling up the gathering to fit.

For the skirt

1 Gather the skirt backs to fit the yokes, then attach them, using 6 mm (¹/₄ in) seams.

2 Pin and baste the smocked front skirt to the front yoke, making sure the stitching is straight above the even smocking pleats.

3 Stitch the skirt side seams and the underarm seams in one go.

4 At the bottom edge of the skirt, stitch two pintucks, 6.5 cm (2¹/₂ in) and 4.5 cm (1³/₄ in) from the edge.

5 Cut three pieces of fabric, each 15 cm x 90 cm (5⁷/₈ in x 35¹/₂ in), for the frill. Join them to make one long strip. Neaten the two raw ends. Make a 6 mm (¹/₄ in) hem on one long edge. On the other long edge, baste a length of the wide Swiss embroidery with both the fabric and the Swiss embroidery facing upwards. Gather them as one. Pin the ruffle to the skirt, adjusting the gathering to fit. Stitch, then neaten the seam.

6 Neaten the raw centre back edges and press them to the wrong side. Sew press studs down the back edge, fixing the hem at the same time. Neatly attach the wider ribbon for ties at the edges of the smocking. Run the narrower cream satin ribbon through the entredeux to gather up the sleeve ends.

Gloria's tips
for Successful Smocking

Smocking pleaters make light work of pulling up the pleats for smocking. An even easier way to get the job done is to use the pleating service provided by stores.

When putting the fabric through a smocking pleater, the right side of the fabric should face the floor of the pleater.

Before using your smocking pleater, run a piece of waxed lunchwrap through it. This will lubricate the needles and allow the fabric to pass through more easily. Only use the number of needles you actually need.

When you have cut the stranded thread, separate the six strands and put them back together in two groups of three strands. Knot them together at the cut end. This process will eliminate tangling and twisting of the thread.

It is important to straighten the edges of the fabric you are going to smock by pulling threads. Fabrics cut on the grain will pleat more easily than those cut against the grain.

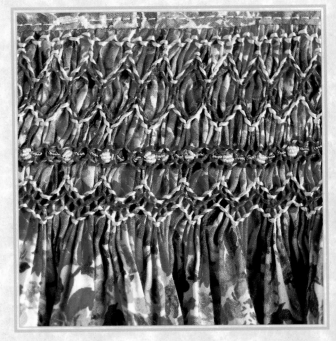

Usually, the smocked piece is tied off 2.5–4 cm (1–1¹/₂ in) smaller than the finished piece will be, otherwise the smocking will need to be stretched too much and may cause ripples when it is attached. Remember to use a reef knot when you tie off your smocking.

Velvet-covered Coathanger

MADE BY FAY KING

This splendid coathanger would make the perfect gift for a bride,
or for a friend 'who has everything'.

Materials

- ❧ wooden coathanger
- ❧ 50 cm (20 in) of cotton velvet or velveteen
- ❧ 1 m (40 in) of 12 mm ($^1/_2$ in) wide rayon ribbon in each of four colours
- ❧ 2.2 m ($2^1/_4$ yd) of green silk ribbon
- ❧ strips of wadding for wrapping the coathanger
- ❧ 50 cm (20 in) of Pellon
- ❧ thread to match the rayon ribbons
- ❧ 1 m (40 in) of cord to match the velvet or velveteen
- ❧ Piecemaker crewel needle, size 9
- ❧ Piecemaker tapestry needle, size 22
- ❧ Piecemaker straw needle, size 8
- ❧ Madeira silk thread, Ecru
- ❧ Mill Hill beads to match the ribbons
- ❧ 35 cm (14 in) of 7 mm ($^5/_{16}$ in) wide ribbon to match the velvet or velveteen
- ❧ sewing thread to match the velvet or velveteen

Method

See the Pattern on Pull Out Pattern Sheet 4.

For the ribbon roses

1 Thread the needle with a thread to match the ribbon. Fold the ribbon at right angles approximately 15 cm (6 in) from the left-hand end. Following the arrow, fold the long part of the ribbon behind the first fold (Fig. 1).

2 Following the arrow in figure 2, fold the ribbon up behind the triangle and hold it firmly in place.

3 Following figure 3, fold the ribbon to the right.

4 Following figure 4, fold the upper end down. Make sure you hold it all firmly together. Continue folding in this way until all the 15 cm (6 in) of the ribbon is folded. Still holding the folded ribbon firmly, gently pull the longer end of the ribbon. Do not pull it too hard or you will lose the centre of your rose and its lovely shape.

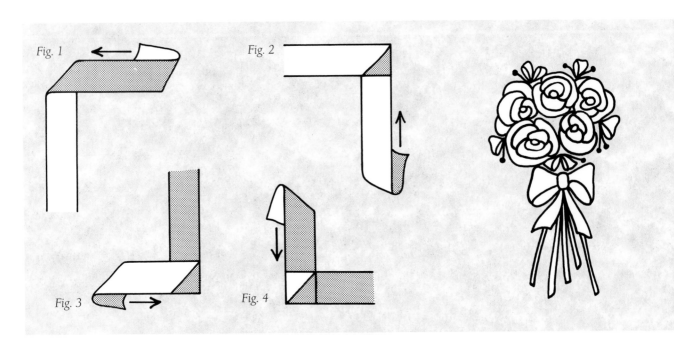

5 Stitch through the centre to the base and around the base to secure the folds of the rose. Cut the rose off from the length of ribbon and set it aside. Make sufficient roses for your posy.

6 Using the pattern, cut one piece of the velvet or velveteen on the bias for the front. Stitch the roses to the velvet in a posy arrangement. Sew three to five beads into the centre of each rose, stitching each bead through the centre of the rose to the back of the velvet to secure.

7 Thread the green ribbon into the tapestry needle and make green ribbon loops around the edges of your posy. Stitch five straight stitch stems.

8 Tie a bow with your chosen ribbon, leaving a long tail. Hand-sew the bow to the base of the roses. Thread each tail of the bow into the tapestry needle and take it to the back of the velvet.

9 Using two strands of the Madeira silk thread and the crewel needle, stitch a few pistol stitch tendrils around the posy.

Assembling

1 Using the pattern, cut one piece of velvet on the straight for the back and two pieces of Pellon.

2 Baste a piece of Pellon to the wrong sides of the front and back of the coathanger. With the right sides together, stitch from the notch at the bottom to the notch at the top. Leaving 1 cm (³/₈ in) open at the centre top, stitch to the other bottom notch. Turn the velvet to the right side.

3 Fold the 7 mm (⁵/₁₆ in) ribbon in half and, with the matching thread, topstitch down both sides. Remove the hook from the coathanger and slip it into the ribbon.

4 Wrap the coathanger in wadding strips, moving from end to end and making sure that each end is well covered. Push a small amount of wadding into each end of the coathanger cover, then pull the cover over the coathanger. Close the opening with a ladder stitch.

5 Starting at the hole at the top, carefully hand-sew the cord around the coathanger seam. Screw in the hook and tie a small bow with the 7 mm (⁵/₁₆ in) wide ribbon.

Shoe Stuffers

MADE BY FAY KING

Perfect companions for the coathanger, these shoe stuffers can be scented with the addition of some lavender to the filling.

Materials

- ❧ 25 cm (10 in) of velvet or cotton velveteen
- ❧ 20 cm (8 in) of lining fabric to match the velvet or velveteen
- ❧ 100 cm (39 in) of 12 mm ($1/2$ in) wide rayon ribbon in each of two colours
- ❧ 120 cm (48 in) of 2 mm ($1/16$ in) wide green silk ribbon
- ❧ 25 cm (10 in) of Pellon
- ❧ rayon ribbon for ties
- ❧ Mill Hill beads to match the rfbbons
- ❧ threads to match the ribbons
- ❧ Piecemaker crewel needle, size 9
- ❧ Piecemaker tapestry needle, size 22
- ❧ 1.25 m ($1^1/3$ yd) of cord to match the velvet or velveteen
- ❧ lavender for filling
- ❧ polyester fibre fill

Method

See the Pattern on Pull out Pattern Sheet 4.

1 Using the pattern, cut two pieces of velvet or velveteen on the bias for the front and two pieces on the straight for the back.

2 Using the pattern again, cut four pieces of Pellon for the 'toe' sections.

3 For each shoe stuffer make and attach three ribbon roses from the rayon ribbon, following the instructions for ribbon roses given on page 112. Complete your arrangement with green silk ribbon loops.

4 Using the pattern lines for the lining, cut four pieces of lining. Stitch one piece at the straight end of each velvet or velveteen piece with the right sides facing and using a 6 mm ($1/4$ in) seam allowance.

5 Lay one piece of Pellon on the wrong side of each velvet piece and baste them together. With right sides together, stitch each pair together from the edge of the lining around the 'toe' to the other edge of the lining. Turn the shoe stuffer to the right side. Fold the lining into the centre and secure the lining on each side seam to hold it in place.

6 Hand-sew the cord over the seam with small stitches, taking it over the lined edge into the shoe stuffer.

7 Fill the toe firmly with the polyester fibre fill, adding approximately 2.5 cm (1 in) of lavender in the middle. Fill up to the dotted line.

8 Run a gathering thread around at the dotted line. Pull the thread up firmly to gather and close the shoe stuffer. Finish with a beautiful bow.

Crazy Quilt

This magnificent old quilt is a perfect example of a style of quilt which was most popular in the last quarter of the nineteenth century.

Such quilts were made using foundation pieces of fabric which were the size of the finished block. This piece was covered, in an apparently haphazard way, with fabrics of every kind – especially silks and satins – and then heavily embellished with embroidery, silks and laces. Fabrics from men's ties, cravats and waistcoats were frequently used, because they had a special richness of colour that added great depth to the work.

In the Victorian era, middle class parlours were full of clutter, and the crazy patchwork style was seen to reflect this mood both in its irregularity and its opulence.

To make your own crazy patchwork quilt, gather up a collection of suitable fabrics, such as silks, satins, velvets, taffetas, moirés, jewel-coloured prints, laces, tulles . . . and as many unwanted men's ties as you can muster. The patchwork technique is exactly the same as for the purse on page 118, but clearly the scale is larger. Use as many embroidery stitches as you can; the greater variety adds to the random appearance. There are some additional embroidery stitches provided for you to use on page 120. Traditionally, the embroidery included animal and bird designs, flowers and leaves, and almost always a spider web complete with spider.

When your quilt top is assembled, complete it as you would any other quilt, but take great care with any pressing you do.

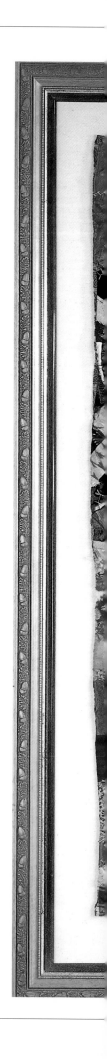

Crazy Quilt Purse

STITCHED BY JUDITH MONTANO

This lovely patchwork purse has been richly embellished with embroidery, sequins, special buttons and charms. Judith's work and her use of colour are quite exceptional. Adding your own embellishments to the basic design will make it unique to you.

Finished size (closed): 14 cm x 18 cm (5¹/₂ in x 7 in)

Materials

- ❧ scraps of silk, satin and cotton fabrics
- ❧ 30 cm (12 in) of velvet, ultrasuede or heavy moiré or other suitable fabric
- ❧ 18 cm x 30 cm (7 in x 12 in) of homespun
- ❧ 18 cm x 30 cm (7 in x 12 in) of iron-on interfacing
- ❧ 30 cm (12 in) Pellon
- ❧ silk buttonhole twist or embroidery floss in an assortment of colours
- ❧ metallic threads
- ❧ beads, buttons, brass charms
- ❧ 3 m (3¹/₄ yd) each of cord in four or five assorted colours and thicknesses
- ❧ three large buttons
- ❧ water-soluble marker pen
- ❧ tacky glue

Method

See the Pattern on Pull Out Pattern Sheet 4.

1 Cut out the pattern pieces from the homespun, interfacing and velvet, ultrasuede or moiré as instructed on the pattern.

Note: When cutting pattern piece A from the homespun, allow an additional 12 mm (¹/₂ in) all around. This piece will be trimmed after all the embellishments are added.

2 Begin creating the patchwork from the centre of the piece. From a dark solid fabric, cut a five-sided shape. Pin it to the approximate centre of the homespun piece A.

3 From another fabric, cut a rectangle that will cover one edge of the centre piece. Lay this piece on the centre piece with the right sides together and stitch in a 6 mm (¹/₄ in) seam. Trim the seam allowance back to 3 mm (¹/₈ in). Press the rectangle back.

4 Working clockwise around the centre piece, continue adding rectangles until each side of the centre piece has been stitched (Fig 1). Trim the free edges to create new angles and five new sides (Fig. 2). Continue to add pieces, keeping a balance of colour, texture, prints and plains.

5 When the homespun is covered, place pattern piece A over it and mark the shape with the water-soluble pen.

6 Stitch assorted laces and ribbons onto the patchwork piece. Cover all the seam lines with embroidery stitches, following the stitch guide on page 120, then sew on the beads, buttons and charms.

Assembling

1 Fuse the interfacing to the wrong side of the patchwork piece, the wrong side of the velvet, ultrasuede or moiré piece A and the wrong side of the velvet piece B.

2 Lay the velvet piece A on the table, facing upwards. Place the quilted piece on top, face down, then the Pellon. Pin the layers together. Stitch around the edge in a 1 cm (³/₈ in) seam, leaving a 5 cm (2 in) opening on one side. Trim the seam allowance, then turn the piece through to the right side. Slipstitch the opening closed. Press.

3 Place the two velvet pieces B together with the right sides facing and a piece of Pellon on top. Pin, stitch, turn and press as for the A piece.

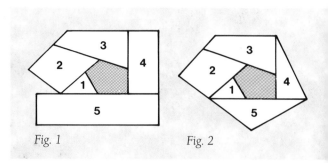

Fig. 1   *Fig. 2*

4 Whipstitch the front and back together as shown on the pattern.

5 Whipstitch a length of cord along the edge of the flap, making a loop in the centre for the closure.

6 Braid the rest of the cords together to make a 140 cm (55 in) length. Tie the ends together, leaving approximately 5–8 cm (2–3 in) below the knot for a tassel.

7 Lay a narrow bead of glue around the edge of the purse. Pin the cord over the glued edge with the tassel at the bottom. Allow the glue to dry, then whipstitch the cord into place.

8 Sew one button at each side of the top and one button to close the purse.

Stitch Guide

Buttonhole stitch

Feather stitch

Cretan stitch

Herringbone stitch

Chevron stitch

Straight stitches with small beads

Embroidered Pillow

STITCHED BY FAY KING

The delicate colour of the fabric is reflected in the charming embroidery to create this elegant little pillow.

Materials

- ♣ 50 cm (20 in) of grosgrain moiré fabric
- ♣ DMC Stranded Cotton: Shell Pink 225, Green 3052, Antique Violet 3041, Lemon 745, Blue 800, White, Ecru
- ♣ straw needles, sizes 8 and 9
- ♣ Piecemaker tapestry needle
- ♣ 2 m (2¼ yd) of 12 mm (½ in) wide soft silk or rayon ribbon
- ♣ 2 m (2¼ yd) of cord
- ♣ 3 m (3¼ yd) of 4 mm (³⁄₁₆ in) wide silk ribbon
- ♣ pencil or water-soluble marker pen
- ♣ sewing thread for basting

Method

See the Alphabet on Pull Out Pattern Sheet 4.

Embroidery

1 Cut a 30 cm (12 in) square from the fabric. Find the centre of the square by folding the fabric into quarters. Measure and mark points along the folds 10 cm (4 in) from the centre point. Join these points together to make a square. Mark the outline of this square with a line of basting.

2 Carefully pin the rayon ribbon around the marked square, tying a bow at each corner. Where the ribbon ends meet, thread the ends into a tapestry needle and take them through to the back of the work, passing the needle and one end through the other. It is a neater effect if you do this close to one corner. Hold the ribbons and bows in place with French knots, stitched in two strands of Ecru, using the size 8 straw needle.

3 In three corners of the square, embroider a different arrangement of flowers, following the stitch guide on

Fig. 1

Fig. 2

Fig. 3

Fig. 4

page 124. In the fourth corner, trace the appropriate initial. Stitch the initial in a neat stem stitch, using two strands of embroidery thread. Work over the stem stitch in an even satin stitch, using two strands of thread and the size 8 straw needle. Embroider a spray of forget-me-nots around the initial.

Assembling

1 Cut a second square, 30 cm (12 in), from the fabric. Place this piece and the embroidered piece together with right sides facing. Stitch around 6 mm ($^1/_4$ in) from the edge, leaving an opening for turning. Turn the cover to the right side, ensuring that all the corners are neat and square.

2 Beginning at the opening, whipstitch the cord in place around the cover, using matching thread, crossing the cord ends and passing them into the opening. Whipstitch around the cord again – this time with the silk ribbon. Slipstitch the opening closed.

Stitch Guide

All the roses, lavender and daisies are combinations of bullion stitches worked in appropriate colours. For the bullion stitch instructions, see the stitch guide on page 11.

Roses

Using six strands of DMC 225 and a size 3 straw needle, make three bullions side by side for the centre of the rose.

Using six strands of DMC Ecru, make five bullions, working clockwise around the centre and beginning each bullion inside the previous one.

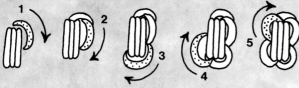

Using six strands of DMC Ecru and a size 3 straw needle, make seven bullions, working clockwise around the centre, in the same way as those made in step 2.

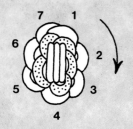

Leaves

a Using three strands of DMC 3052 and a size 6 straw needle, make a bullion from **a** to **b** with nine wraps. Ease them off the needle, then give the thread a tug which will tighten the wraps and taper the bullion. Take the needle to the back of your work at **c**.

Make a second bullion with eight wraps beside the first one and finish it in the same way.

Small rosebud

b Using three strands of DMC 225 and a size 6 straw needle, make one bullion with ten wraps, stitching from **a** to **b**.

Using three strands of DMC Ecru and a size 6 straw needle, make one bullion with twelve wraps on either side of the centre.

Using three strands of DMC 3052 and a size 6 straw needle, make one bullion with fourteen wraps on either side. Tug the thread a little to taper the end. Work three tiny satin stitches across the bottom at **a**.

Lavender stems

Work the stems in stem stitch, using two strands of DMC 3052 and a size 8 straw needle.

Gloria's tip: To maintain a graceful curve with stem stitch, always keep the thread to the outside of the curve.

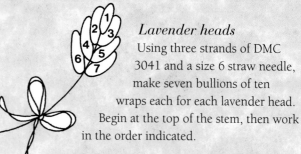

Lavender heads

Using three strands of DMC 3041 and a size 6 straw needle, make seven bullions of ten wraps each for each lavender head. Begin at the top of the stem, then work in the order indicated.

For the bow, bring narrow silk ribbon through from the back of the work and tie a bow at the front.

Daisies

Using two strands of DMC Ecru and a size 8 straw needle, make twelve bullions with ten wraps each, working from the centre outwards in the order indicated in the diagram. Position the petals so that there is room for a lemon bullion with six wraps at the centre. Make the bud in the same way, following the diagram on the right.

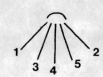

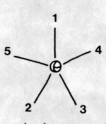

Forget-me-nots

Using three strands of DMC 800 and a size 6 straw needle, make five satin stitch petals in the order indicated on the diagram on the left. For each petal, stitch three or four times from **a** to **b** as shown in the diagram on the right.

Make a French knot in the centre, using two strands of DMC 745 and a size 8 straw needle.

Teddy Bear

MADE BY ROSE HILL

This cuddly little teddy is sure to become a much loved friend. For a really authentic feel, make the teddy bear from plush fur fabric.

Materials

- 🍀 15 cm x 50 cm (6 in x 20 in) of fur fabric
- 🍀 felt or suede for the paw pads and inner ears
- 🍀 five pairs of wooden disc joints with split pins and washers
- 🍀 tracing paper
- 🍀 fineline marker pen
- 🍀 small sharp scissors or a craft knife
- 🍀 embroidery thread, Black
- 🍀 two small black beads or buttons for the eyes
- 🍀 extra-strong sewing thread
- 🍀 polyester fibre fill
- 🍀 small sharp scissors
- 🍀 extra-long needle
- 🍀 small pliers
- 🍀 satin ribbon for a bow

Method

See the Pattern on Pull Out Pattern Sheet 2.

1 Trace the pattern pieces from the Pattern Sheet. Transfer all the markings to your tracings, cut out the pieces and use them as your pattern.

2 Place the patterns on the wrong side of the fur fabric, making sure that the pile of the fur fabric is always in the direction of the arrows. Draw around each pattern piece with the marker pen. Check that all the pairs match up, then cut out all the pieces, labelling each one.

Hint: When you are cutting out the fur fabric, make sure that you cut only the woven backing not the fur pile. It is easier to do this properly if you use small sharp scissors or a craft knife.

3 With the right sides together, sew the side heads together under the chin, from the nose to the neck. Sew on the centre head, beginning at the nose and sewing from the nose down one side to the back neck. Begin at the nose again and sew down the other side of the head.

4 Sew a strong gathering thread around the neck edge. Turn the head to the right side. Stuff the head firmly with the polyester fibre fill.

5 Put one split pin through a washer, then through a wooden disc. Place them inside the head and draw up the gathering around the protruding split pin. Tie a knot to secure the gathering.

6 Stitch one paw pad to the right side of each short arm piece. Place the short and long arm pieces together with right sides facing and stitch around the outside edge, leaving an opening as indicated. Turn the arms to the right side.

7 Fold the leg pieces over double with the right sides together. Sew around the outside edge, leaving an opening as indicated.

8 Baste one foot section to each leg, check the fit, then stitch each foot in place. Turn the legs to the right side.

9 Push another split pin through a washer and a wooden disc, then push the pin through each limb from the inside to the outside at the point marked.

10 Stuff the limbs firmly with the fibre fill, then close the openings, stitching with the strong thread.

11 Sew one side body to the centre body, stitching from the neck down. Sew on the other side body in the same way, but continue the stitching around the centre back as far as the marked opening. Sew the centre back from the neck to the opening. Gather the neck edge with the strong thread, draw up the gathering and secure it. Turn the body through to the right side.

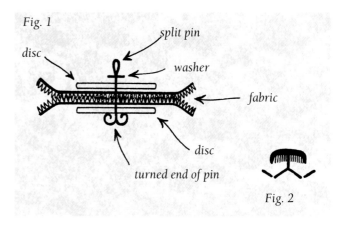

Fig. 1
split pin
disc
washer
fabric
disc
turned end of pin
Fig. 2

12 To attach the head, push the split pin through the gathered neck opening of the body, then push the pin through a wooden disc inside the body. Using the pliers, open out the pin and push each arm firmly over on to the disc to hold the head firmly in place (Fig. 1).

13 Position the arms and the legs on the body at the points indicated. Check that all the limbs are facing in the correct direction before securing the pins as for the head.

14 Stuff the body firmly with the fibre fill, then slipstitch the opening closed.

15 Place two ear pieces together with the right sides facing. Stitch around the curved edge, leaving the straight edge open. Turn the ears to the right side. Pin them in place on the sides of the head, then stitch them in place with the strong thread.

16 Trim the fur on the muzzle, then embroider the nose following figure 2.

17 With the long needle and the strong thread, stitch from the back of the head through to the position of the right eye. Thread the button or bead on to the needle, then pass the needle through the top of the muzzle to the position of the left eye and thread the second button or bead. To secure the eyes, take the needle through the head to the back of the head and secure the thread.

Note: If you are making this bear for a very small child, it is safer to embroider the eyes.

18 Trim excess fur from around the eyes and across the top of the muzzle, then tie a satin bow around the bear's neck.

DECOUPAGE

Découpage dates back at least as far as the seventeenth century when the fascination with all things oriental was at its height. Demand for hand-painted furniture from China was so great, the supply could not keep up. It was discovered by enterprising cabinet makers, that hand-coloured pictures could be stuck to the surface of wooden furniture and so submerged beneath layers of lacquer that they could pass for the real thing.

These days, enthusiastic découpeurs do not have to spend time hand-colouring prints for découpage (unless they want to, of course). Not only do old books, maps and calendars ensure the availability of images for découpage, but there are books and papers produced specifically for the purpose.

It is possible to apply découpage to just about any flat surface, providing it is clean and in reasonable condition. Lidded boxes of all shapes and sizes are great favourites for découpage. In this section, there are two boxes, each one treated in a slightly different style. The Découpage Box on page 130 is covered all over with images – even the bottom is decorated. The Postcard Box on page 138 has découpage only on the lid, with a single dominant image of the postcard surrounded by flowers.

The three-fold screen on page 134 is découpaged with a profusion of dolls and teddy bears. The effect of all those faces is quite extraordinary and contrasts with the simplicity of the découpage on the brooches on page 140. If you've always wanted to try découpage, these brooches would be a wonderful introduction to this delightful craft.

Découpage Box

MADE BY NERIDA SINGLETON

This box is a beautiful example of découpage – the creative composition of paper cutouts on a surface which is then covered by numerous applications of clear varnish, allowing the image to glow through.

When découpaging a box, always keep the focus of the design on the top and front of the box with less emphasis on the bottom and sides. The background can be painted, covered with wrapping paper or constructed from pictures.

Materials

- ❧ box (with the fittings removed)
- ❧ curved cuticle or surgical scissors, finely pointed
- ❧ 10 cm/4 in rubber roller
- ❧ 2.5 cm/1 in imitation sable brush for varnish
- ❧ Liquitex Gloss Medium and Varnish OR Atelier OR Matisse MM7 OR Jo Sonja Gloss Medium Varnish for Découpage for sealing
- ❧ Clag School Paste and PVA adhesive
- ❧ Goddard's Cabinet Makers Polish
- ❧ Wattyl Danish Wax (optional)
- ❧ sponge applicator or cheap brush for sealer and gesso
- ❧ gesso
- ❧ glass paper
- ❧ wet and dry sandpapers, 280, 600, 1200 and 2000 aluminium oxide
- ❧ clear varnish (various brands of varnish and polyurethanes will do)
- ❧ tack cloth
- ❧ steel wool, 0000
- ❧ Blu-Tack or Faber Castell's Tackit
- ❧ oil-based colouring pencils: sepia, black
- ❧ sponge and towel
- ❧ protective mask and goggles
- ❧ mineral turpentine and brush cleaner
- ❧ beeswax stick or wood putty
- ❧ Scotchbrite scourer
- ❧ brass fittings
- ❧ sheets of no. 10 white cardboard
- ❧ 3M microfine or micromesh finishing kits
- ❧ artists acrylic paints (if you are painting a background), and sea sponge
- ❧ black fineline permanent marker pen OR gold fineline permanent marker pen
- ❧ workable fixative (optional)
- ❧ waxed paper
- ❧ plastic zip folders
- ❧ rubber or cork block
- ❧ scalpel or paring knife
- ❧ muslin cloth
- ❧ craft glue
- ❧ spray adhesive
- ❧ spatula
- ❧ wadding
- ❧ fabric for the lining
- ❧ cutting compound
- ❧ electric drill and 2 mm/ $^1/_{16}$ in drill bit
- ❧ ribbon

Method

Preparation

1 Mark the top and bottom of the inside of one side of the box so that it will fit flush when hinged. Check for crevices which may need to be filled with the beeswax stick or wood putty. Apply the filler with the spatula. If you are using putty, be generous with it because it will shrink as it dries. Beeswax is preferable for filling as it does not shrink.

2 Sand the box well with glass paper, then sand it lightly with no. 280 wet and dry sandpaper and wipe it clean.

3 If you wish, you can apply the gesso before lightly sealing the box or you can paint the background with at least two coats of artists acrylic paints, applying each coat in a different direction. If you are not applying gesso or painting the background, eliminate step 3.

4 Seal the box with your choice of sealer, drawing the sealer out well so that no bumps and lumps are evident. Seal the inside and rims of the box as well.

5 Seal the images sparingly on both sides of the paper before cutting them out. Seal the back of the picture first. Allow it to dry for ten to fifteen minutes, then sparingly seal the front of the picture.

6 Cut out each picture precisely, eliminating the inside areas you don't need before cutting the outline. Cut with the curve of the scissors pointing away from the picture. Remove all the white background at the edges of the image.

7 Make a cardboard template for each surface of the box. Using the Blu-Tack, experiment with the design, beginning with the focal picture and building up the complementary images until you are satisfied with the effect.

Note: Pictures which cover a corner and travel down the sides will have to be mitred at the corners. Make sure you have enough pictures before you begin gluing.

Gluing

1 Using a 3:1 mixture of Clag paste and PVA apply a generous amount to the box surface and smear it with your fingertips until it is silky. Before placing the pictures down, make sure that you have not missed any areas and that there are no hard lumps of glue. Place the first picture, then massage with a little extra glue on top of the picture until the glue becomes tacky and the bonding between the picture and surface takes place. Distribute the glue evenly behind each picture.

2 Add a little more glue, then using the rubber roller, roll with very gentle pressure from the centre of the picture out to the edges. Don't use too much pressure when you are rolling as this will eliminate all the glue and you will have no adhesion. Hold the surface up to the light to check if there is any accumulated glue or air behind the picture. Keep the roller clean by wiping off built-up glue.

3 Using a damp sponge, wipe any excess glue from the surface of the picture. The glue will appear dull when held in the light. Do not glue over a wet picture.

4 Repeat steps 1 to 4 until all the pictures have been glued down. Check that there are no dull patches.

5 Allow the box to dry, then check each picture for white edges. Colour any that you find with an appropriately coloured oil-based pencil and smudge the edge if the line is too definite. This will allow all the images to blend together.

6 Sign and date your work with the marker pen. If you are using a gold fineline pen, spray your signature sparingly with workable fixative when the ink is dry, otherwise it will smear under the sealer. Allow the fixative to dry.

7 Seal all the surfaces sparingly. If you are not able to finish gluing and have to leave the project overnight, clear away all the glue, pencil any edges, then seal the object. This will prevent the pictures from losing adhesion, especially at the corners, and also alleviates the possibility of damage. (Vermin are instantly attracted to the excess glue on the pictures.)

8 If you do not use all the sealed pictures, place them between sheets of waxed paper and file them into plastic zip folders. The sealer will stick them together if you don't use the waxed papers to separate them.

Varnishing

1 Use the protective mask and have good ventilation in the area in which you are working, when you are varnishing. Using the fine brush, beginning applying the varnish at the top, using light sweeps in one direction. Do not stir the varnish or polyurethane unless so advised in the manufacturer's instructions. Satin, matte and water-based products should be thoroughly stirred to incorporate the sediment. Gloss is a harder and more suitable product.

2 Be sure to brush out any accumulation of varnish where the top and sides of the box join or at the rims. Check for drips. Wipe the excess varnish from the brush on to the side of the varnish tin. Using the tip of the brush, lightly sweep across all the surfaces to remove any air bubbles and excess varnish. Be sure to work in a good light. Support both sections of the box raised on tins to allow the air to circulate around them while they dry.

3 Allow twenty-four hours drying time between each coat of varnish. Before applying the next coat of varnish, wipe the surface dust particles off with the tack cloth. Alternate the direction of each coat of varnish.

4 When you have applied twenty coats, begin sanding with the no. 600 wet and dry sandpaper. Sand lightly in one direction with the wet sandpaper wrapped around a rubber or a cork block. Wipe off the white residue with the damp sponge then allow the box to dry. Colour any white edges, then seal the surfaces and begin varnishing again.

5 Repeat the process of sanding with the no. 600 wet and dry sandpaper and varnishing until the surface is quite flat. This may take somewhere between thirty and fifty coats of varnish.

6 Change to no. 1200 sandpaper for the final polishing after the last three coats of varnish have been applied. Remove the excess build-up of varnish at the rims of the box using a scalpel or paring knife. Be sure the surface is uniformly dull – that there are no crevices between superimposed pictures which show tendrils of gloss. If there is still gloss evident, rub with a dry Scotchbrite, then with the steel wool. A cutting compound is also helpful at this stage.

7 For a gloss finish, apply a light coat of varnish, using seven parts varnish to three parts mineral turpentine. Be sure there are no air bubbles in the surface and place the object in a dust-free environment to dry. Repeat this process until the surface is perfectly smooth.

8 For a waxed finish, put a teaspoon each of clear beeswax and the Goddard's polish in an oven to warm them, or in a microwave oven for about twenty seconds on HIGH. Apply the polish sparingly with the dampened muslin cloth and work on only small sections at a time. Dip the cloth in boiling water and buff each section before you move on to the next one. Repeat if necessary. Apply a final light coat of the polish over the entire surface and repeat this often during the curing time to enhance the finish even further. It can take from six to twelve months for an object to harden completely.

Finishing

1 Using the electric drill and 2 mm/ $^1/_{16}$ in bit, secure the brass corners. Avoid fittings which are secured with nails – those with screws are the most suitable. Use the drill bit for all the fittings, starting with the corners. Work on the handle and then the top. You will find it easier to manipulate the fittings before the hinges are attached.

To attach the hinges, measure an equal distance from the ends and drill the opposite sides in sequence. Add the clasp – choose one that has a padlock. It is best to secure the top of the clasp and then line up the underneath section to ensure it is not too loose. An antique padlock and handles can add a great deal of style to a box.

2 If you have not taken the pictures over the rim, paint the inside of the box rims with artists acrylic paints. Leave to dry, then apply two coats of sealer, allowing time for the paint to dry between each coat.

Lining

1 Cut ten cardboard shapes for templates, remembering to allow for the thickness of the fabric at each side. Cut 6 mm/ $^1/_4$ in of wadding the same size as the top and bottom templates. Lightly spray the cardboard with the spray adhesive and stick the wadding to the cardboard.

2 Cut the fabric 1.5 cm/ $^3/_4$ in wider than the template all around. Mitre the corners by cutting a triangle from each corner of the fabric to allow it to fit flush at the corners when glued. Glue the edges of the fabric to the back of the cardboard with craft glue. Apply the craft glue to the bottom of the box, spreading it evenly with a spatula. Place the fabric-covered template on to the glue and weight it down to ensure adhesion.

3 Now that the thickness of the cardboard, wadding and fabric is determined in the top and bottom of the box, reduce the width of the cardboard templates accordingly for all the sides. The length of the sides will also need to accommodate two thicknesses of extra fabric so keep readjusting them. Do not pad the sides as this will reduce the interior space of the box. Attach the fabric-covered side pieces in the same way as for the top and bottom, but omitting the wadding. Work on each side separately. Secure the sides with craft glue keeping pressure on them until they are firmly stuck. Glue a length of ribbon behind the covered cardboard on one end to hold the box lid open. It is a good idea to do these two ends last.

4 If your box is round or oval with the lip of the lid fitting over the base, make a pencil line around the base of the lip on to the bottom and only paste the pictures to this line. Successive coats of varnish will build up and prevent the lid from fitting properly. The bare areas can be painted in a colour to match the background colour of the pictures or in a colour which coordinates with the lining.

Nerida Singleton has written three découpage books:

♣ *Découpage*, Boolarong Publications, Brisbane 1990
♣ *Découpage, An Illustrated Guide,* Sally Milner Publishing, 1991
♣ *Découpage Designs,* Sally Milner Publishing, 1992, and a calendar
♣ *Découpage Calendar,* Five Mile Press & Sally Milner Publishing, 1993

Découpage Screen

MADE BY GLORIA MCKINNON

Découpage is enjoying a worldwide revival. This charming paper craft reached its zenith in Europe in the nineteenth century and is bringing a touch of the romance of those times to today's busy world. This three-panel screen stands approximately 95 cm (38 in) high and shows off the beautiful découpage perfectly. You can, of course, découpage any hard surface, such as a box, tray or placemat.

Materials

- ❧ three-panel hinged wooden screen
- ❧ wet and dry sandpaper, 400 grade and 600 grade
- ❧ Liquitex Gloss Medium & Varnish for sealing
- ❧ wrapping paper
- ❧ pictures for découpage
- ❧ paintbrush
- ❧ Clag paste
- ❧ PVA glue
- ❧ plastic ice-cream container with lid
- ❧ rubber roller
- ❧ small curved scissors
- ❧ cotton cloth
- ❧ sponge brush
- ❧ Conte oil-based brown pencil
- ❧ Feast Watson Polyurethane Varnish
- ❧ synthetic golden sable brush, 2.5 cm
- ❧ tack cloth
- ❧ thinner
- ❧ glass jar with plastic lid
- ❧ coloured pencils
- ❧ steel wool, 0000
- ❧ beeswax polish

Method

Preparation

1 Remove the hinges from your screen and store them away carefully as it may be some time before they will be replaced.

2 If the screen is not smooth, sand it lightly with the no. 400 wet and dry sandpaper. Wipe off all the dust. Apply two coats of the Liquitex Gloss Medium & Varnish in opposite directions on both sides of the screen.

3 In the plastic container, mix three parts Clag to one part PVA adhesive to form a smooth paste.

4 To provide a background for the cut-out pictures, this screen has been covered with wrapping paper. You can cover the front and the back with wrapping paper, if you are going to découpage the back of your screen as well as the front. Before gluing down the wrapping paper, seal both sides, then use the roller to smooth out the paper and to remove any air bubbles. Remember to stagger the joins in the wrapping paper. The joins are quite simple to cover with large pictures but you want to avoid having all the large pictures in a row. Once the screen is completely covered, be sure to remove any excess glue with a damp cloth. Seal the wrapping paper with two coats of sealer, alternating the direction of each one.

Note: You can create a background for your pictures in a number of ways: You can paint the surface with several coats of acrylic paint, you can cover the entire surface with cut-out pictures, or you can cover it with a sheet of good quality wrapping paper.

5 Choose the pictures you are going to use for your découpage. Using the sponge brush and Liquitex sealer, seal them on both sides, before you cut them out. Most prints need to be sealed, although very good publications, such as art books, do not. Set the pictures aside to dry.

6 Cut out the pictures, making sure that the curved edges of the scissors are facing outwards as you cut. Remove all the white edges or background from around the pictures – the white edges become very obvious when varnished.

7 Always have enough pictures cut out before you begin gluing. Decide on your focal picture for each panel and place it in position, then work outwards. Arrange the pictures, moving them around until you are pleased with the composition.

Gluing

1 Apply a generous amount of the glue mixture to your screen (but not the prints), position the print in its desired location and apply more glue to the top of the print. Using the roller, start from the middle of the print and roll outwards in all directions to squeeze out the excess glue and air bubbles. Do not press too hard or there will not be enough glue left under the prints. Wipe all the glue from the roller immediately after use.

2 Using the damp sponge or cloth, wipe over the surface of the prints to remove the excess glue, then check in the light for air bubbles or excess glue under the prints. If they are present, add more glue to the top of the print, then use your thumb to smooth the bubbles out towards the closest edge. Wipe again, then continue adding more shapes until you have completed your design. Leave until completely dry.

3 When you have finished, check all the edges of the prints to make sure that no white edges are showing. If there are some, apply the oil-based pencil to the edges, smudging it with your fingers.

4 Cover with two coats of sealer, working in alternate directions for each coat.

Varnishing

1 Using the sable brush, apply a light coat of varnish. Allowing at least twelve hours for each coat to dry, apply one coat each day preferably. Wipe down with the tack cloth to remove the dust before each coat, and apply each following coat in the opposite direction to the previous one.

2 Clean the brush in the thinner, suspending the brush through the plastic lid of the glass jar so that it doesn't touch the bottom. Change the thinner when it turns cloudy.

Sanding

1 After you have applied twenty coats of varnish, sand your screen to remove any bumps and to even out the crevices. Continue sanding in one direction only, using the 400 grade sandpaper, until the varnish surface is level. Take care with edges and corners. If you accidentally sand off any paper, touch it up with a coloured pencil.

2 Lightly sand in between each of the next forty-odd coats of varnish using the 600 grade sandpaper, removing the dust each time with the tack cloth.

3 When the varnishing is completed and everything feels smooth, apply a final coat of varnish in a dust-free environment.

4 If you desire a waxed finish, rub over the surface with grade 0000 steel wool to reduce the shine, then vigorously apply a wax polish. Replace the hinges.

Postcard Box

MADE BY GLORIA McKINNON

Découpage with a difference: this oval box features an old postcard which gives it a nostalgic air.

Materials

- ❧ wooden box
- ❧ paper to cover the box lid
- ❧ postcard
- ❧ pictures for cutting out
- ❧ curved cuticle scissors, finely pointed
- ❧ rubber roller
- ❧ 10 cm (4 in) imitation sable brush for varnishing
- ❧ Liquitex Gloss Medium and Varnish
- ❧ Clag paste
- ❧ PVA adhesive
- ❧ two sponge applicators or cheap brushes (for sealer and paint)
- ❧ clear varnish
- ❧ acrylic paint, Black
- ❧ paint thinner
- ❧ wet and dry sandpaper, 400 grade and 600 grade
- ❧ kitchen cloth, such as Chux
- ❧ tack cloth
- ❧ craft knife (optional)
- ❧ the box circumference plus 1 m (40 in) of 3 cm (1¹/₄ in) wide wired ribbon
- ❧ 1 m (1¹/₈ yd) of 3 mm (³/₁₆ in) wide satin ribbon

Method

1 Coat the box with two coats of Liquitex to seal it, then paint the sides of the box and the lid rim with two coats of Black paint.

2 Cut the exact shape of the lid top from the paper for covering the lid. The fit must be exact, but if it is a bit larger than the lid, you can trim it with a craft knife when all the glue is absolutely dry. Mix three parts Clag to one part PVA adhesive and glue the paper to the top of the lid. Massage it with your fingers to make sure that no bubbles of air or glue remain under the paper. Using the rubber roller with a light pressure, roll from the centre of the lid out to the edges. Wipe off any excess glue to keep the roller clean.

3 Paint the front of the postcard with six coats of Liquitex, alternating the direction with each coat.

4 Soak the postcard in water for approximately thirty minutes. Remove the postcard from the water and place it face down on a clean surface. Rub vigorously on the wrong side with the kitchen cloth until the postcard is quite thin. Blot it dry, then leave it to dry completely.

5 When the postcard is quite dry, glue it onto the box lid, using the three parts Clag paste to one part PVA adhesive. Make sure the glue mixture is evenly distributed behind the picture. Using the rubber roller with light pressure, roll from the centre of the postcard out to the edges Wipe off any excess glue to keep the roller clean.

6 Cut out your pictures and arrange them around the postcard. Glue them on in the same manner as the postcard. Wipe any excess glue off the surface with a damp cloth each time, so that there is no build-up. Allow the glue to dry, then seal the lid with two coats of Liquitex.

7 Using the sable brush, begin to apply light coats of varnish to the lid, leaving each coat to dry for twelve hours. Ideally, you should apply one coat a day, alternating the direction of each one. Wipe down the box between coats of varnish with the tack cloth. Clean the brush in paint thinner, suspending the brush through the lid of a jar of the thinner so that the brush does not touch the bottom. Change the thinner when it turns cloudy.

8 After you have applied twenty coats of varnish, sand the surface with the 400 grade sandpaper to remove any irregularities.

9 Lightly sand between the next forty-odd coats of varnish, using the 600 grade sandpaper and removing the dust each time with the tack cloth.

10 When the varnishing is completed and the surface feels quite smooth, apply the two final coats of varnish in a relatively dust-free environment.

11 Apply two coats of varnish to the sides of the box and the rim of the lid.

To attach the ribbon

Fold the wider ribbon in half lengthwise. Placing the halfway point at the join in the lip of the lid, glue the ribbon around the lip. Tie the ends into a bow at the front, incorporating the finer ribbon into the bow.

Découpage Brooches

MADE BY KARA KING

What could be more romantic than a brooch featuring roses or a Victorian beauty, made using a technique popular in that era.

Choosing the right image is crucial for making this brooch. Consider carefully the size or the picture and whether you wish to use one large picture or several small ones. Enthusiastic découpeurs are always on the lookout for interesting pictures they can store away for just the right project.

Materials

- ❧ wooden brooch (oval or round)
- ❧ brooch back
- ❧ suitable images
- ❧ FolkArt Acrylic BaseCoat
- ❧ gold paint
- ❧ Liquitex Sealer
- ❧ craft glue
- ❧ rubber roller
- ❧ fine-pointed sharp curved scissors
- ❧ Clag paste
- ❧ PVA adhesive
- ❧ clear varnish
- ❧ paintbrushes
- ❧ brushes for sealer and glue
- ❧ sable brush for varnish
- ❧ wet and dry sandpaper, 600 grade
- ❧ tack cloth

Method

1 Paint the front and back of the brooch with two coats of acrylic paint, allowing the paint to dry thoroughly between coats.

2 Mix three parts of Clag to one part of PVA adhesive, making sure the mixture is quite smooth with no lumps. Spread some of the glue mixture on the brooch, then place the image or images on the glued surface. Add a little more glue to the face of the image, spreading it with your fingers to test for lumps. Using the rubber roller, gently roll from the centre out to the edges. Remove any excess glue from the roller.

3 Using your finger, rub a little gold paint around the edge of the brooch.

4 When the glue and the paint are quite dry, coat the face of the brooch with two coats of Liquitex Sealer.

5 Using the sable brush, apply at least twelve coats of varnish, each one in the opposite direction to the last, and allowing twelve hours between the coats. It is also a good idea to wipe the brooch with a tack cloth between coats to remove all traces of dust.

6 Sand the brooch lightly with the wet and dry sandpaper to remove any bumps and ridges. Wipe with the tack cloth, then apply two coats of varnish in as dust-free an environment as you can manage. Finally, glue on the brooch back with the craft glue.

QUILTING

Quilts were originally made by frugal and practical pioneer women from re-covered fabrics to provide warm covers for the family's beds. Later, with the growth of America's cotton industry and the manufacture of relatively inexpensive cotton fabrics, quilts took a new turn – still practical, they now took on a decorative aspect.

From these humble beginnings, quilts have evolved, until today we have a continuing and growing interest in traditional quiltmaking, alongside contemporary quilters who use their craft as an avenue of personal and artistic expression.

The ready availability of wonderful fabrics, increasingly produced specifically for quiltmaking, and the burgeoning of quiltmaking groups and guilds, have led to a tremendous increase of interest in quiltmaking. This interest has been further fuelled by the growing acceptance of quilts as art and, more and more, we are seeing quilts in art galleries.

The quilts in this book, with the exception of the Silk Baby's Quilt on page 170, are all based on traditional designs. The Seven Sisters Quilt on page 144 is made entirely from scraps of Liberty fabric. Machine-pieced and machine-quilted, the Twilight Garden Quilt on page 148 is very quick to make. Three of the quilts: Baby's Spring Garden on page 151, Postcards from the Past on page 154 and the Hearts and Hands wallhanging on page 158 are all pieced over papers in the English manner and hand-quilted. The wallhanging also features appliqué and embroidered mottos of love and friendship. The Floral Flavours Quilt on page 163 is a special favourite with its sunny colour and all-over stipple quilting.

As with most skills, there are valuable quilting tricks and short cuts to be learned. On page 166, you will learn a foolproof method for piecing the Double Wedding Ring Quilt.

Seven Sisters Quilt

STITCHED BY FAY KING

This quilt design has been popular for more than a hundred years. Made in this way, it is not a quilt which is usually recommended for beginners as it does require a little experience to piece it accurately.

It is very important to ensure your templates are traced precisely from the ones given on the pattern sheet so that your quilt comes together well.

In our quilt, each star and border is cut from a different Liberty print fabric – a total of seventy-three different fabrics. For simplicity, it is possible to piece each hexagonal unit from the same seven fabrics and one background fabric.

This quilt has been handpieced by the English method, using cardboard throughout, and handquilted.

Finished size: 133 cm x 150 cm/52 in x 60 in

Materials

- ❧ scraps of seventy-three different fabrics
- ❧ 1.5 m/1²⁄₃ yd of white homespun for background
- ❧ fineline permanent marker pen
- ❧ template plastic
- ❧ scissors
- ❧ medium-weight cardboard
- ❧ sharp pencil
- ❧ transparent ruler
- ❧ masking tape
- ❧ handsewing needles
- ❧ strong matching sewing thread
- ❧ approximately 145 cm x 160 cm/58 in x 64 in of backing fabric
- ❧ approximately 138 cm x 156 cm/55 in x 62 in of wadding
- ❧ quilting thread

Method

See the Templates on Pull Out Pattern Sheet 1.

Cutting

Cut out the following pieces:
For each star: six of template A in floral fabric.
For each hexagonal unit: seven stars (forty-two of template A in floral fabric, thirty of template A in the background fabric and six of template B in the background fabric, six of template C in the colour of your choice) and piece them.
For the quilt top: four each of templates D, E, F and G from the background fabric.

1 Trace template A from the pattern sheet on to the template plastic, using the marker pen. Cut out the template along the marked line.

2 Using the plastic template A and the sharp pencil, draw around the template on to the cardboard. Cut out the cardboard templates in the numbers you require.

3 Place the plastic template A on the various fabrics and draw around the outside edge with the pencil. This pencil line is the sewing line. Cut out the fabric pieces, adding a 6 mm/¼ in seam allowance all around each piece.

Piecing

1 Centre a cardboard template on the wrong side of a fabric piece. Turn the seam allowance over on to the cardboard, folding in the corners to form a mitre.

2 Thread a sewing needle and knot the end of the thread. Beginning in the centre of one side of the diamond, baste the seam allowance together around the diamond. (Fig. 1)

3 When all the diamonds have been prepared in this way, you are ready to begin joining them together. Place two diamonds together with right sides facing and the edges even. Diamonds are joined by overcasting across the two adjoining edges of both diamonds. Always choose a sewing thread that matches the darker of the two fabrics you are working with.

Beginning 6 mm/ $\frac{1}{4}$ in from the left-hand end of the side you want to sew, work to that end, then down the whole side to the other end, then work backwards for 6 mm/ $\frac{1}{4}$ in. (Fig. 2). This method ensures a very secure join which will not come undone. Cut off the thread, leaving a short tail. Take care not to stitch through the cardboard. Piece six matching diamonds together in this way to make the star.

4 Following the block diagram given on page 147, piece all the stars together with the background pieces to form a complete hexagonal unit. Make nine such units. The cardboard should bend quite easily, making your piecing more comfortable to hold as the work grows bigger.

5 Trace and cut the fabric and cardboard, using template C. Baste template C fabric pieces over the cardboard as for the diamonds. Join the template C pieces to each side of the hexagonal unit, using the same method of piecing as for the stars.

6 Following the construction diagram on page 147, lay all the units with the background pieces D, E, F and G on the floor or some other suitable surface. Experiment with the arrangement of the hexagonal units until you are pleased with it, then piece all the elements to form the quilt top.

7 Measure the length of the quilt top through the centre. Cut two 11 cm/4 $\frac{1}{2}$ in wide fabric borders to this length plus 12 mm/ $\frac{1}{2}$ in for seam allowances. Cut the cardboard to size without seam allowances. If you need to join cardboard to achieve this length do so by butting the edges together – do not overlap them – and secure them with masking tape. Join the side borders in the same way as the stars were pieced. Make the top and bottom borders in the same way.

8 When the quilt top is assembled, remove all the basting and the cardboard. Press well.

9 On the outside edges, redo the basting so that there is a 6 mm/ $\frac{1}{4}$ in basted hem all around the quilt top.

Quilting

1 Lay the backing fabric face down on a suitable surface and tape it in place so it does not move. Place the wadding on top and then the completed quilt top on top of that. Note that the backing fabric and the wadding are both bigger than the quilt top – these will be trimmed later. (Fig. 3)

2 Baste from the centre diagonally out to the edges and then in the lines indicated in the diagram. (Fig. 4) Baste around the edges.

3 Quilt the quilt top as you please. Quilting around the stars, hexagonal units and borders is very simple and attractive. Stop the quilting 2.5 cm/1 in from the edges.

4 When the quilting is complete, trim the wadding to the same size as the quilt top.

5 Trim the backing to be 2 cm/ $\frac{3}{4}$ in bigger than the quilt top. Fold under this 2 cm/ $\frac{3}{4}$ in so that it sits on the front of the wadding between the quilt top and the wadding. Slipstitch the folded edges together.

Don't forget to sign and date your quilt on the back.

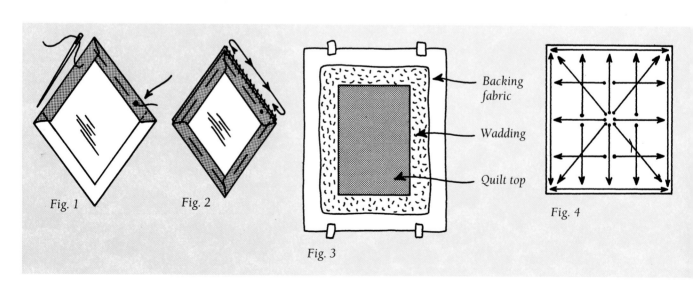

Fig. 1   Fig. 2

Backing fabric

Wadding

Quilt top

Fig. 3

Fig. 4

Block Diagram

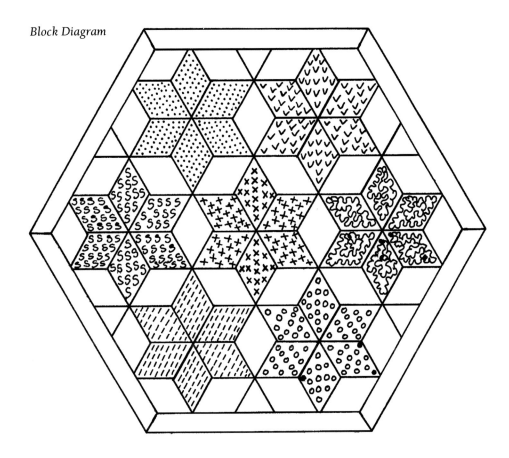

Construction
Diagram

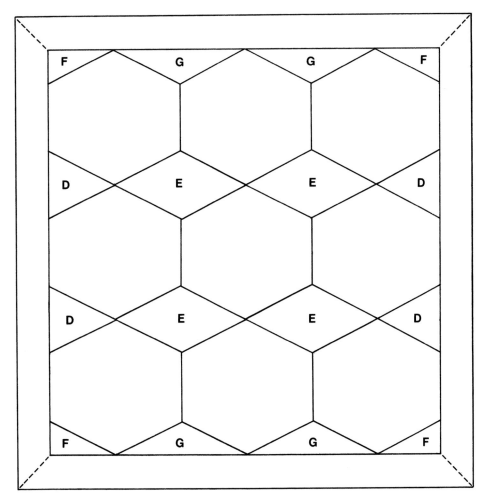

Twilight Garden Quilt

STITCHED BY YAN PRING WITH THANKS TO MARY ELLEN HOPKINS

This is a quick little quilt to make. Machine-pieced and machine-quilted, it simply uses star blocks set on the diagonal, with floating triangles to complete the edges.

You can piece the star blocks with different fabrics for the star points or use the same fabric. The instructions given here are for using the same fabric, but do not be afraid to experiment to achieve a special effect or to include a favourite scrap. It is best to choose the fabrics for the borders after you have pieced the stars in order to determine what colour will work best with the overall scheme.

Finished size: 104 cm x 125 cm/41 in x 49 in

Materials

- ♣ 1.2 m/1⅓ yd of background fabric
- ♣ 40 cm/½ yd of fabric for the star points
- ♣ 20 cm/¼ yd of fabric for the star centres
- ♣ 20 cm/¼ yd of striped fabric for the inner border
- ♣ 10 cm/4 in of fabric for the middle border
- ♣ 60 cm/¾ yd of floral fabric for the outer border
- ♣ 45 cm/18 in of fabric for the binding
- ♣ 1.3 m/52 in of fabric for the quilt backing
- ♣ 110 cm x 130 cm/44 in x 52 in of wadding
- ♣ transparent ruler
- ♣ sharp pencil
- ♣ scissors, or Olfa cutter and self-healing mat
- ♣ pins
- ♣ matching sewing threads
- ♣ masking tape

Method

See the Construction Diagram on Pull Out Pattern Sheet 1.

Cutting

Note: 6 mm/¼ in seam allowances are included in all the measurements. Be exact with your seam allowances, otherwise the quilt will not come together well. It is a good idea to place all the pieces into piles marked A, B, C, D, E.

Cut out the following pieces:
From the background fabric: Seventeen squares (A), 11 cm x 11 cm/4¼ in x 4¼ in; forty-eight rectangles (B), 7.5 cm x 11 cm/3 in x 4¼ in; four squares (C), 23 cm x 23 cm/9 in x 9 in, cut into quarters diagonally; three squares (D),18 cm x 18 cm/7 in x 7 in , cut into quarters diagonally; two squares (E), 11 cm x 11 cm/4¼ in x 4¼ in, cut in half diagonally.

From the star point fabric: one hundred and forty-four squares 4.5 cm x 4.5 cm/1¾ in x 1¾ in.

From the star centre fabric: eighteen squares 7.5 cm x 7.5 cm/3 in x 3 in.

From the striped border fabric: four 4.5 cm/1¾ in wide strips across the full width of the fabric.

From the middle border fabric: four 2.5 cm/1 in wide strips across the full width of the fabric.

From the floral border fabric: four 14.5 cm/5¾ in wide strips across the full width of the fabric.

Piecing

1 Lay one of the star point squares in the upper left-hand corner of one of the background rectangles B with the right sides together and the raw edges even. Stitch across the diagonal. (Fig. 1) Trim off the upper triangle of the star point square and press the remaining triangle over to the right side. (Fig. 2)

2 Make twenty-four such rectangles with a triangle in two corners (Fig. 3) and twenty-four with four triangles. (Fig. 4)

3 Assemble the quilt, following the construction diagram. First assemble diagonal strips (including the triangles at the ends) until you have all thirteen strips as numbered on the diagram and press. Next, join the strips together horizontally and press. Press the quilt top well.

For the borders

1 For the striped inner border, join the two side borders first, then trim them to fit the edges of the quilt top. Attach the top and bottom borders in the same way. Press.

2 Attach the middle border and then the outer border in the same way. Press. (Fig. 5)

Quilting

1 Lay the backing fabric face down on a suitable surface and tape it in place so it does not move. Place the wadding on top and then the completed quilt top on top of that. Note that the backing and the wadding are both bigger than the quilt top – these will be trimmed later.

2 Baste from the centre out to the edges and then in the lines indicated in the diagram. (Fig. 6) Baste around the edges.

3 Machine-quilt following the diagonal lines of the piecing. The two narrow borders are quilted in the ditch, following the seams.

4 Handquilt the floral border in a random pattern, outlining the flowers in the print.

5 When the quilting is completed, trim the backing and the wadding to the same size as the quilt top.

Binding

1 Cut six 7 cm/3 in wide strips of the binding fabric. Join the six strips to achieve the required length.

2 Fold the strip over double with wrong sides together and raw edges even. Press.

3 Pin the binding around the right side of the quilt with the raw edge of the binding 6 mm/¼ in from the quilt edge. Stitch in a 6 mm/¼ in seam.

4 Press the binding over to the back of the quilt and either machine-sew or handsew the binding in place.

Don't forget to sign and date your quilt on the back.

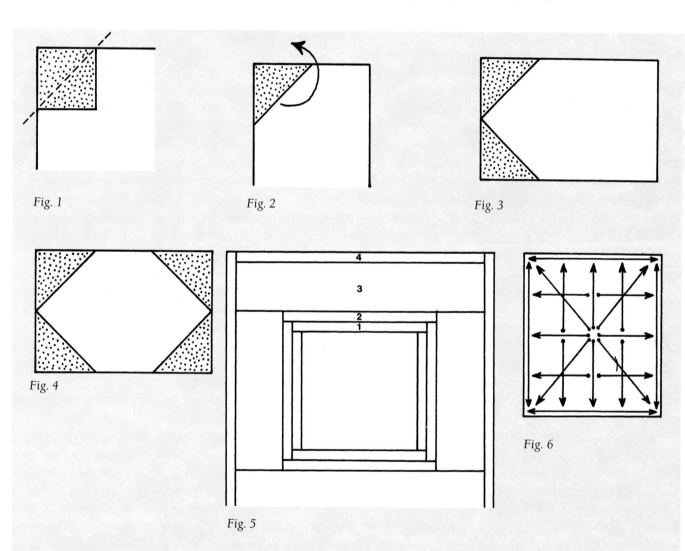

Fig. 1

Fig. 2

Fig. 3

Fig. 4

Fig. 5

Fig. 6

Baby's Spring Garden

STITCHED BY FAY KING

This pretty cot quilt shows another variation of the traditional nine-patch design. It is a true scrap quilt in which the lovely Liberty scraps are not arranged, but have been chosen at random.

Materials

- scraps of cotton Liberty print fabrics, big enough to cut 5 cm (2 in) squares
- 1 m ($1\frac{1}{8}$ yd) of white homespun
- 50 cm (20 in) of fabric for the border
- 150 cm (59 in) of backing fabric
- cot-sized wadding
- crewel needles, size 9
- quilting needles, sizes 8 to 9
- cotton thread, White
- quilting thread, White
- tracing paper
- fineline permanent marker pen
- template plastic
- sharp pencil
- transparent ruler
- medium-weight cardboard
- scissors
- transfer paper

The quilt has been hand-pieced by the English method, using cardboard throughout. It has also been hand-quilted.

Finished size: approximately 149 cm x 89 cm (59 in x 35 in)

Method

See the Templates and the Quilting Designs on Pull Out Pattern Sheet 2.

6 mm ($\frac{1}{4}$ in) seam allowances are included in the measurements, except where you are asked to add them on.

Cutting

1 Using the marker pen, trace template A from the pattern sheet on to the template plastic. Cut out the template along the marked line. Do the same with templates B, C and D. Set them aside.

2 Using the plastic template A and the sharp pencil, draw and cut out three hundred and sixty cardboard templates.

3 Using the plastic template A and the sharp pencil, draw two hundred floral squares and one hundred and sixty white squares. Cut out the squares, adding a 6 mm ($\frac{1}{4}$ in) seam allowance all around each piece.

Piecing

1 Place a cardboard template A on to the back of each fabric square. Turn the seam allowance over on to the cardboard, folding the corners straight over.

2 Thread a sewing needle and knot the end of the thread. Beginning on one side of the square, baste the seam allowance together around the square (Fig. 1). When all the squares have been prepared in this way, you are ready to begin joining them together. Place two squares together with right sides facing and the edges even. Squares are joined by overcasting across the two adjoining edges. Always use a thread that matches the darker of the two fabrics.

Beginning 6 mm ($\frac{1}{4}$ in) from the left-hand end of the side you want to sew, work to that left-hand end, then down the whole side to the other end, then work backwards for 6 mm ($\frac{1}{4}$ in) (Fig. 2). Take care not to stitch through the cardboard. This method ensures a very secure join which will not come undone. Cut off the thread, leaving a short tail. Piece forty nine-patch blocks with five floral squares and four white squares, selecting the floral squares at random and only changing your selection if you happen to pick up two squares of the same fabric for the same block (Fig. 3).

For the quilt top

1 Using plastic template B, cut twenty-eight squares of cardboard. Cover each of these squares with white fabric in the same way as for the small squares. Cover twenty-two triangles made from template C and four triangles made from template D with white fabric in the same way.

2 Piece the nine-patch blocks with the white squares in diagonal rows, adding one triangle C at the end of each

row and one triangle D at the four corners of the quilt top
(Fig. 4). Use the same method of piecing as for the nine-patch
blocks.

For the borders

1 Carefully measure the length of the quilt, measuring
through the centre. Cut 5 cm (2 in) wide lengths of
cardboard to this measurement. Draw a line 5 cm (2 in) from
each end, then draw the diagonal out from this line to make
the mitred corners (Fig. 5). If you need to join the cardboard
to achieve the length you require, butt the edges together and
tape them without overlapping.

2 Cut strips of the border fabric 6.2 cm (2½ in) wide. You
will have to join fabric to cover the length of the
cardboard. Take care to place the join in the centre. Cover the
cardboard with the border fabric in the same way as before
and attach the borders to the sides of the quilt.

3 Make the top and bottom borders in the same way. Sew
the borders to the quilt edges. Remove all the basting
and the cardboard.

4 On the outside edges of the quilt, redo the basting so
there is a 6 mm (¼ in) basted hem all around the quilt.

Quilting

1 Lay the backing fabric face down on a suitable surface.
Place the wadding on top, then place the completed quilt
top on top of that, face upwards. Note that the backing fabric
and the wadding are both bigger than the quilt top – these
will be trimmed later (Fig. 6).

2 Baste from the centre, diagonally out to the edges and
then in the lines indicated in the diagram (Fig. 7). Baste
around the edges.

3 Trace the butterfly and the flower quilting patterns from
the pattern sheet and transfer the designs to the white
squares, alternating flowers and butterflies. Hand-quilt the
designs. Quilt around the squares in the nine-patch blocks,
then quilt around the quilt in the lines indicated (Fig. 8).

Finishing

When the quilting is completed, trim the wadding to the size
of the quilt top. Trim the backing to be 2 cm (¾ in) bigger
than the quilt top. Fold under this 2 cm (¾ in) so that it sits
between the wadding and the quilt top. Slipstitch the folded
edges together.

Don't forget to sign and date your quilt on the back.

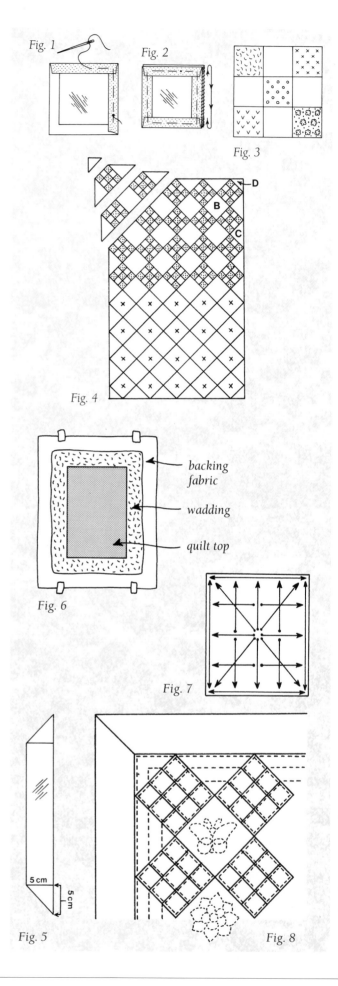

Fig. 1

Fig. 2

Fig. 3

Fig. 4

backing fabric

wadding

quilt top

Fig. 6

Fig. 7

5 cm

5 cm

Fig. 5

Fig. 8

Postcards from the Past

STITCHED BY FAY KING

This quilt is reminiscent of the quilts which were made in the middle of the last century, using a 'conversation' fabric. This is a fabric, often with a large print, which has many points of interest and can be successfully used in large areas. In this quilt, the conversation fabric has been used in the bands which separate the nine-patch blocks.

The quilt has been machine-pieced and hand-quilted.

Finished size: 150 cm x 165 cm (59 in x 65 in)

Materials

- ✿ 50 cm (20 in) of each of two floral fabrics
- ✿ 50 cm (20 in) of each of two plain fabrics
- ✿ 1 m (1⅛ yd) of print fabric for the triangles
- ✿ 2 m (2¼ yd) of conversation fabric
- ✿ 50 cm (20 in) of fabric for the binding
- ✿ 3.4 m (4 yd) of backing fabric
- ✿ 155 cm x 170 cm (61 in x 67 in) of cotton wadding
- ✿ matching sewing thread
- ✿ scissors, or Olfa cutter and self-healing mat
- ✿ transparent ruler
- ✿ tracing paper
- ✿ sharp pencil
- ✿ quilting thread
- ✿ quilting needles (size 8 for beginners, size 10 for the more experienced)

Method

See the Templates on Pull Out Pattern Sheet 2.

6 mm (¼ in) seam allowances are included in all the measurements.

1 Cut the floral and the plain fabrics into 5 cm (2 in) strips, cutting across the full width of the fabric. Join three strips of each floral/plain fabric combination into the strip sets shown in figure 1, making two of set 1 and one of set 2 for each fabric combination.

2 Cut the selvages of both ends of each strip set, then cut them into 5 cm (2 in) sections (Fig. 2).

3 To form the blocks, join the sections made in step 2 as shown in figure 3, taking care to match the seams. Make twenty-three blocks of one fabric combination and twenty-two blocks of the other one. Press the blocks carefully.

4 Trace and cut out the triangle templates from the pattern sheet. Using Template A, cut out eighty triangles. Using Template B, cut out twenty triangles. Join an A triangle and a B triangle to opposite sides of each nine-patch block (Fig. 4). Press carefully.

5 Join nine of these nine-patch block and triangle combinations together into vertical rows, alternating the floral fabrics. Make three rows beginning with one fabric combination and two rows beginning with the other one. Join a B triangle at the ends of the rows to square them up. Press the rows carefully, taking care not to stretch the outer edges of the triangles which are on the bias.

6 Measure the length of the rows, measuring through the centre. Cut four 13 cm (5 in) wide strips of the conversation fabric to this length. Join the pieced rows, alternating with the bands of the conversation fabric. Take care to alternate the two types of pieced rows as well.

For the borders

1 Measure the length of the quilt top, measuring through the centre. Cut 14 cm (5½ in) wide side borders to this length. Sew on the side borders.

2 Measure the width of the quilt top, measuring through the centre. Cut 14 cm (5½ in) wide top and bottom borders to this length. Sew on the top and bottom borders. Press the quilt top well.

Quilting

1 Cut the backing fabric in half lengthwise. Cut off the selvages on the inner edges, then rejoin the two halves to achieve a backing of the desired width.

2 Place the backing face down with the wadding on top and the quilt top on top of that, face upwards. Baste all the layers of the quilt sandwich together, beginning at the centre and working out to the edges. Baste around the outside edges (Fig. 5).

3 In keeping with the traditional look of this quilt, it has been hand-quilted quite closely in the patterns indicated (Fig. 6).

4 When the quilting is completed, trim the wadding and the backing to the size of the quilt top.

Binding

1 Cut eight 6.5 cm (2½ in) wide strips across the full width of the fabric. You will need to join two strips together to reach the length required for each side of the quilt.

2 Press the binding over double with the wrong sides together and the raw edges even. On the right side of the quilt, sew the binding to the edges of the quilt (sides first, then the top and bottom) with the raw edges even. Turn the binding to the back of the quilt and slipstitch it in place, neatening the corners.

Don't forget to sign and date your quilt on the back.

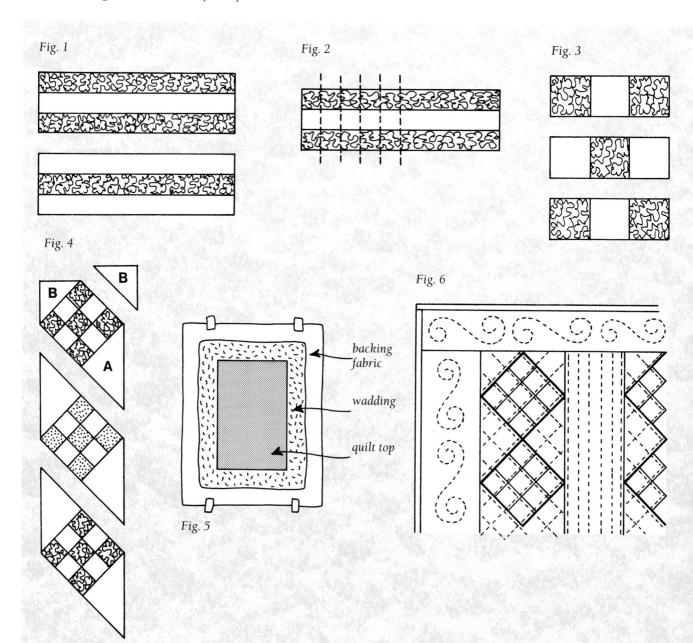

Fig. 1

Fig. 2

Fig. 3

Fig. 4

Fig. 5

backing fabric

wadding

quilt top

Fig. 6

Gloria's tips
for Successful Hand-quilting

Unlike most machine-quilting, which is often designed to be functional and virtually invisible, hand-quilting is often the most admired feature of a quilt. As a general rule with hand-quilting, if you place your fist on the quilt top, you should touch quilting on all sides.

Quilting patterns can come from a variety of sources, including stencils or patterns from books such as this one. The best way to transfer a pattern from a book to your quilt top is to trace it first on to white paper. Then, using a waterproof laundry marker, trace the design on to a piece of tulle. Now, you can simply pin the tulle into the appropriate spot and draw over the design with a water-soluble fabric marker pen. The design will appear on your fabric as a series of tiny dots. The tulle can be used over and over again.

When you are using a water-soluble marker pen, never mark more than you can quilt at one sitting, and always wash the markings off in cold water as soon as the section is quilted.

To quilt in really straight lines, use masking tape. Position the tape from point to point and you will have a nice straight edge to quilt along. When you have finished that row, simply pull up the tape and place it in position for the next row.

If the quilting motif that you love is really a bit small for where you wish to use it, quilt another line 6 mm (¼ in) outside the motif. Not only will this make it larger, it will also make the design stand out even more.

If you are unsure which design will suit your quilt – angular or rounded, cut out a paper template and lay it in position on the quilt top. It will give you the effect of a quilted shape without you having to stitch and unpick.

Hearts and Hands

STITCHED BY FAY KING

This wallhanging is a lovely gift for a special friend or for a new baby. Embellished with mottoes of love and friendship, it has been hand-pieced and hand-appliquéd, but it could be machine-pieced, if you prefer.

Note: If you are hand-piecing, draw the templates accurately on cardboard and cut them out carefully. If your templates are accurate, your pieces will fit together well. Always place the templates square on the fabric. Take particular care to ensure that the corners are neat and square, basting them carefully before stitching.

Pieces are joined by overcasting across adjoining edges. Place the pieces together with right sides facing. Beginning 6 mm (¼ in) from the left-hand end of one side, stitch down to that end, then along the full length of the side, then work backwards for 6 mm (¼ in). This creates a very strong join.

Use 6 mm (¼ in) seam allowances throughout.

Finished size: 58.5 cm x 73.5 cm (23 in x 29 in)

Materials

- ♣ 1 m (1⅛ yd) of homespun fabric for background
- ♣ small pieces of a variety of print fabrics
- ♣ cotton thread to match the fabrics
- ♣ stranded embroidery thread in a variety of colours
- ♣ 20 cm (8 in) of fabric for each border
- ♣ 75 cm (30 in) of backing fabric
- ♣ 75 cm (30 in) of Rayfelt or light wadding
- ♣ quilting thread
- ♣ Piecemaker crewel needles, size 9, for embroidery
- ♣ Piecemaker between needles, size 9, for quilting
- ♣ cardboard for templates
- ♣ pencil and ruler
- ♣ tracing paper
- ♣ scissors for cutting cardboard and another pair for cutting fabric

Basic Method for Hand-appliqué

1 Cut the shape required from the cardboard, taking care that all the edges are smooth.

2 Using the cardboard shape as your pattern, cut out the fabric piece with a 6 mm (¼ in) seam allowance all around.

3 Baste the fabric over the cardboard by turning the seam allowance over onto the back of the cardboard. Clip into curves and corners and pleat the fabric where necessary to allow the fabric to turn smoothly.

4 Appliqué the piece onto the background fabric using tiny invisible stitches.

Method

See the Templates, the Assembly Diagrams and the Layout Diagram on Pull Out Pattern Sheet 3.

Block 1

1 Trace the templates. Cut out all the elements from cardboard, then from fabric, using a 6 mm (¼ in) seam allowance.

2 Appliqué the centre heart onto the square of background fabric, then cut as indicated on the template.

3 Piece the heart from the elements shown. When the heart is completed, appliqué it onto an 18 cm (7 in) square of background fabric. Embroider the motto around the heart.

4 Cut a 15.25 cm (6 in) square of cardboard. Using this as your template, cut out the fabric with a 6 mm (¼ in) seam allowance all around. Baste the fabric over the cardboard.

Block 2

1 Trace the templates. Cut out all the elements from cardboard, then from fabric, using a 6 mm (¼ in) seam allowance.

2 Appliqué the heart on the wall, then embroider the motto. It is easier to handle this way. Piece the house as shown in the assembly diagram.

Block 3

1 Trace the template. Using the template, draw the heart onto a piece of homespun.

2 Cut a five-sided piece of fabric and baste it to the centre of the heart.

3 Join on the other fabrics, overlapping the centre piece and embroidering the joins in a variety of stitches as shown.

4 Using the template, cut out a cardboard heart. Baste the pieced heart over the cardboard heart. Press well, then appliqué it onto the centre of a 16.5 cm (6¹/2 in) square of background fabric.

5 Write your name and the date in pencil, then embroider it in backstitch.

6 Cut a 15.25 cm (6 in) square of cardboard. Baste the fabric square over the cardboard.

Block 4

1 Using the template, cut a cardboard square to size, then carefully cut it into the elements. Use these small pieces as your templates for cutting the fabric pieces, remembering to add 6 mm (¹/4 in) seam allowances all around.

2 Using the small heart template, trace the shape of the embroidery onto the small square piece. Embroider the floral heart, using two strands of embroidery thread. The flower petals are worked by stitching twice into the same two holes. The centre is a French knot.

3 Baste all the elements over the cardboard pieces. Press well, then join the elements in the order indicated on the template. Do not remove the cardboard.

Block 5

1 Trace the templates. Cut out all the elements from cardboard, then from fabric, using 6 mm (¹/4 in) seam allowances all round.

2 Baste the fabric pieces over the cardboard. Press well, then appliqué them onto a 16.5 cm (6¹/2 in) square of background fabric in the following order: heart, hands, feet, dress, then the head.

3 Embroider the hair with French knots. Draw in the motto in pencil, then embroider it.

4 Cut a 15.25 cm (6 in) square of cardboard and, using this as your template, cut out the background fabric with 6 mm (¹/4 in) seam allowances all around. Baste the fabric over the cardboard.

Block 6

1 Using the template, cut a cardboard square to size, then carefully cut it into the elements. Use these small pieces as your templates for cutting the fabric pieces, remembering to add 6 mm (¹/4 in) seam allowances all around.

2 Embroider the motto, then baste all the fabric pieces over the cardboard pieces.

3 Piece the heart and the border, trimming the squares so will all fit together again. Do not remove the cardboard.

Block 7

1 Trace the heart template. Cut it out of cardboard, then out of fabric, using 6 mm (¹/4 in) seam allowances.

2 Baste the fabric over the cardboard. Press well, then remove the cardboard. Appliqué the heart onto a 16.5 cm (6¹/2 in) square of background fabric.

3 For the flowers, cut four pieces of fabric using the template and allowing 6 mm (¹/4 in) for turning under. Turn under the seam allowance, then sew a running stitch around the edge. Pull up the thread tightly to gather the fabric. Tie off the threads, then appliqué the flowers on as for the heart. Sew a small bead or a French knot in the centre.

4 Embroider the motto. Embroider the flower stems in chain stitch, then work the bow in silk ribbon.

5 Cut a 15.25 cm (6 in) square of cardboard. Baste the fabric over the cardboard.

Block 8

1 Cut a 16.5 cm (6¹/2 in) square from the background fabric. Press it into quarters and then along both diagonals to mark the centre.

2 Cut a 12.75 cm (5 in) square of fabric for the star. Press it in the same way as before. Centre this piece over the background square with the centres matching and baste along the pressed lines.

3 Using the template, cut eight hearts from cardboard. Using the cardboard, cut eight hearts from eight different fabrics with 6 mm (¹/4 in) seam allowances all around. Baste the fabric over the hearts.

4 From the centre, mark 3.2 cm (1¹/4 in) along each fold line. Appliqué the hearts in place, placing the point of each heart at one of the marked points. These may need to be adjusted slightly so that they all touch.

5 Cut a 15.25 cm (6 in) square of cardboard. Baste the fabric over the cardboard square.

Block 9

1 Trace the heart template. Cut it out from cardboard, then from fabric with 6 mm (^{1}/$_4$ in) seam allowances all around.

2 Cut out a 16.5 cm (6^1/$_2$ in) square from the background fabric. Appliqué the heart onto the centre of the square.

3 Trace the hand onto the fabric. Cut it out with a 6 mm (^{1}/$_4$ in) seam allowance. Appliqué the hand over the heart, turning the seam allowance under with the point of the needle. Clip between the fingers as necessary.

4 Write in the motto with pencil, then embroider it in backstitch.

5 Cut a 15.25 cm (6 in) square of cardboard. Baste the fabric over the cardboard square.

Block 10

1 Trace the heart template. Cut it out from cardboard, then from fabric with 6 mm (^{1}/$_4$ in) seam allowances all around.

2 Cut out two cardboard templates (each one-quarter of the main square). Using these, cut out two fabric squares with 6 mm (^{1}/$_4$ in) seam allowances all around. Appliqué a heart onto the centre of each of the squares. Baste each square over cardboard.

3 For each small nine-patch square, trace the template (one-quarter of the large square) and cut it from cardboard. Cut the cardboard into nine squares as marked. Using these small templates, cut out nine pieces of fabric with 6 mm (^{1}/$_4$ in) seam allowances all around. Baste the fabric over the squares. Join all the squares together to make the nine-patch square. Make two.

4 Join the four quarters of the block to make the complete block.

Block 11

1 Trace the templates. Cut out all the elements from cardboard, then from fabric with (^{1}/$_4$ in) seam allowances all around.

2 Baste the fabric pieces over the cardboard pieces. Press well, then appliqué them onto a 16.5 cm (6^1/$_2$ in) square of background fabric in the order indicated on the assembly diagram.

3 Draw in the motto, the smoke, the fence and the cloud, then embroider them in backstitch.

4 Cut a 15.25 cm (6 in) square from cardboard. Baste the fabric over the cardboard.

Block 12

1 Trace the heart template. Cut out four hearts from cardboard. Using these as your templates, cut four hearts from fabric with 6 mm (^{1}/$_4$ in) seam allowances all around. Baste each fabric heart over a cardboard heart. Press well, then remove the cardboard.

2 Trace the template, then cut it out from cardboard. Cut the cardboard along the marked lines. Using these pieces as your templates, cut them out from fabric with 6 mm (^{1}/$_4$ in) seam allowances all around.

3 Appliqué a heart into the centre of each square, placing the hearts diagonally as shown. Baste the fabric squares over the cardboard squares.

4 Baste the triangles over the cardboard. Join the corner triangles, then piece the four squares together.

Assembling

1 When all the blocks are completed, join them together in rows of three, following the layout diagram. Join the four rows together.

2 Cut 2.5 cm (1 in) wide strips of cardboard that are 61 cm (24 in) long. Cover these strips with fabric and join them to the sides of the joined blocks.

3 Cut 2.5 cm (1 in) wide strips of cardboard that are 51 cm (20 in) long. Cover these strips with fabric, with 6 mm (^{1}/$_4$ in) seam allowances, and join them to the top and bottom of the joined blocks.

4 Cut 5 cm (2 in) wide strips of cardboard that are 66 cm (26 in) long. Cover these strips with fabric, with a 1.25 cm (¹/₂ in) seam allowance at the edge, and join them to the first border at the sides.

5 Cut 5 cm (2 in) wide strips of cardboard that are 61 cm (24 in) long. Cover these with fabric, with 1.25 cm (¹/₂ in) seam allowances at the edge. Join these to the top and bottom of the first border.

6 Trace the heart template. Using the template, cut one from cardboard, then from fabric with 6 mm (¹/₄ in) seam allowances all around. Baste the fabric over the cardboard. Press well, remove the cardboard, then appliqué the heart in the lower left corner.

7 Remove all the cardboard. Baste the seam allowance under around the edge.

Quilting

1 Cut the wadding and the backing fabric 5 cm (2 in) bigger all around than the top. Lay the backing face down on a table with the wadding on top and the pieced top on top of that, face upwards. Baste the three layers together widthwise, lengthwise, diagonally and around the edges.

2 Outline-quilt around the motifs in the wallhanging. To quilt the hearts in the border, make a template of a heart from clear adhesive paper, such as Contact. Work around the border, placing the heart, quilting around it, then moving it to the next position.

3 On block 5, stitch a small cross for each eye, through all thicknesses.

Gloria's tips
for Successful Hand-appliqué

Finishing

1 Remove all the basting. Cut the wadding to the same size as the top and cut the backing 2.5 cm (1 in) bigger all around. Fold the backing fabric over the wadding and slipstitch the edges together.

2 For the casing, cut a 5 cm (2 in) wide piece of backing fabric. Turn under the raw edges and stitch it to the back of the wallhanging, 1.25 cm (¹/₂ in) from the top and 2.5 cm (1 in) from the edges.

Cutting

Cut the shapes from cardboard so they are smooth, not jagged. To achieve this, it is best to turn both the cardboard and scissors while you cut, and make long cuts, rather than short, choppy ones.

When cutting fabric pieces for hand-appliqué, cut them on the bias wherever possible.

Piecing

All the hand-appliqué for this project has been worked by basting fabric over a cardboard shape. No raw edges of fabric should be visible. Once this step is completed, press the piece with a hot iron to make the edges crisp and sharp. Remove the cardboard, then appliqué the piece onto the background. For the pieced blocks, cut cardboard templates for each element of the design. Baste the fabric over the cardboard, but do not remove the cardboard at this stage.

Appliqué

To appliqué, use a cotton thread in a colour to match the appliqué, not the background. No stitches should be visible from the front of the work, so take small stitches, catching only a few threads of the appliqué piece with each stitch.

Floral Flavours Quilt

STITCHED BY NERYL DURIE

This quilt has been given a distinctive thirties look by using the Aunt Grace's Scrapbag range of fabrics in the blocks and the braided border. To enhance this look even further, use a cotton wadding.

Note: Accuracy is very important in this pattern. If the pieces don't fit correctly or the block won't lie flat, chances are your sewing or cutting has been inaccurate. When piecing, sew only as far as the sewing line and not into the seam.

Finished size: approximately 205 cm x 245 m (81 in x 99 in)

Block size: 30 cm (11³/₄ in)

Materials

Note: All fabrics are 110 cm (44 in) wide cottons
- ♣ 5.2 m (5²/₃ yd) of yellow fabric for the border, setting pieces and binding
- ♣ 2 m (2¹/₄ yd) of white fabric
- ♣ 3 m (3¹/₃ yd) total scraps in 1930s-look prints
- ♣ 100 cm (40 in) of pink fabric
- ♣ 80 cm (32 in) of green fabric
- ♣ 7.2 m (8 yd) of backing fabric
- ♣ 210 cm x 250 cm (83 in x 101 in) wadding (use a fine wadding, if you are going to machine-quilt)
- ♣ wonder thread for machine-quilting
- ♣ cotton thread to match the backing fabric
- ♣ template plastic
- ♣ fineline permanent marker pen
- ♣ safety pins, no. 2 (if you are going to machine-quilt)

Method

See the Templates on Pull Out Pattern Sheet 3.

Cutting

6 mm (¹/₄ in) seam allowances are included.

1 Cut out the following pieces:
From the yellow fabric: four 16.5 cm x 225 cm (6¹/₂ in x 88 in) borders and twelve 31 cm (12¹/₄ in) setting squares (plain blocks).

For the large setting triangles: four 46.5 cm (18³/₈ in) squares. Cut each one diagonally in both directions to make sixteen smaller triangles (two of which will not be used).

For the corner triangles: two 24 cm (9¹/₂ in) squares. Cut each one in half diagonally to make four triangles.

From the remainder of the yellow fabric: 10.5 m (11¹/₂ yd) for the binding.

2 Using the template plastic and the marker pen, trace and cut out templates for pieces A, B, C, D, E, F1. Where F2 is mentioned in the instructions, place the template F1 face down on fabric instead of face up.

Using the templates, cut the following pieces:
From the white fabric: twenty F, twenty F2, sixty C, sixty D, eighty E.

From the 1930s print fabrics: one hundred and twenty A.

From the pink fabric: twenty B.

From the green fabric: one hundred C.

Piecing

Note: The block is easier to assemble if you piece the diamonds in two halves, then join them, rather than joining them all in a circle.

1 Piece three squares by joining a white C and green C to a white D. Make three.

2 Piece two triangles by joining one green C and two E triangles.

3 Piece four A diamonds, then set two pieced squares in the corners to form the centre of the top half of the block.

4 Join two A diamonds and one B cone piece to form the centre of the bottom half of the block. Join one of the pieced squares into the corner, then join the top and bottom halves of the block together. Join the pieced triangles and the F1 and F2 pieces to complete the block. Make twenty identical blocks (Fig. 1).

5 Lay the blocks on point in five horizontal rows of four blocks each. Lay the plain blocks, the large setting pieces on the sides and the corner triangles in place.

6 Piece the blocks in diagonal rows, then join the rows. Press the joined blocks well.

For the borders

1 Cut the floral fabrics for the border into 6.5 cm x 14 cm (2^1/$_2$ in x 5^1/$_2$ in) logs. The braided border can be pieced in a totally random fashion or the fabrics can be repeated in a regular manner. If the latter is your choice, plan your colour and fabric pattern in advance.

2 Arrange the first two logs as shown in figure 3. Place them together with the right sides facing and stitch along the edge indicated in figure 4. Open out the fabrics and press the seam towards piece number 2.

3 Continue to add logs as shown in figure 5 until the piece is long enough for the borders. Sew on the side borders first, then the top and bottom borders.

Note: Do not trim a braided border like this one before you attach it, as the trimming will create bias edges which might stretch. Stitch the border in place first, then trim away the excess fabric. You can even bind the quilt before you trim.

Assembling

1 Cut the backing fabric into three 2.3 m (2^1/$_2$ yd) lengths. Join them to make one piece for the complete backing.

2 Place the backing face down on a table with the wadding on top and the quilt top face upwards on top of that. If you are machine-quilting, pin every 8 -15 cm (3 - 6 in), using the safety pins. If you are hand-quilting, baste the quilt layers together, stitching through the centre vertically, horizontally, diagonally, then around the edges.

Stipple Quilting

Stipple quilting is a form of echo quilting, also known as meandering. It creates a heavily quilted appearance and is often used for backgrounds. The lines of quilting never touch, nor do they cross. The effect can be very small or large and open, and should appear random (Fig. 2).

To stipple quilt, you will need to use the darning foot on your sewing machine. Drop, or cover your feed dogs, whichever your machine requires. The stitch length is controlled by the speed at which you move your fabric under the foot, and the speed of your machine. You need to run the machine fairly fast as the faster you go, the easier it is to quilt. Keep the speed constant: erratic speed can result in uneven stitches.

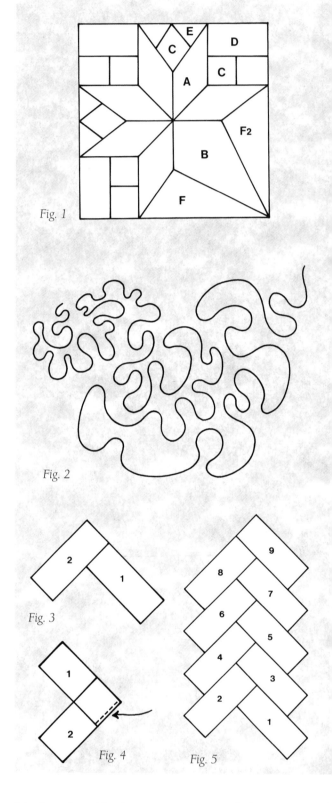

Fig. 1

Fig. 2

Fig. 3

Fig. 4

Fig. 5

Stipple quilting like this is synonymous with the name Harriet Hargrave.

Double Wedding Ring Quilt

STITCHED BY YAN PRING WITH THANKS TO JOHN FLYNN

This quilt pattern has been a favourite of quilters for a very long time. Now, thanks to John's strip-piecing method and special techniques, you can make this quilt more easily than ever before.

You can purchase John's Double Wedding Ring Template Set or you can make your own from the ones we have provided on the pattern sheet.

As there are two colour gradings in this quilt (blue and pink), you will need twelve different fabrics for the arcs, six in each grading. For the corners, you will need two colour combinations, a light and a dark to suit each colour grading from the arcs (four fabrics). Fat quarters are the ideal way to buy all these fabrics.

Finished size: 108 cm (42.5 in) square

Materials

- ❧ 1.1 m (1^1/$_8$ yd) of background fabric
- ❧ fat quarters for the arcs and corners
- ❧ 1.25 m (1^1/$_3$ yd) of fabric for the backing
- ❧ 1.25 m (1^1/$_3$ yd) of wadding
- ❧ 75 cm (30 in) of fabric for the binding
- ❧ coloured pencils
- ❧ cutting mat
- ❧ rotary cutter
- ❧ ruler
- ❧ matching sewing thread
- ❧ quilting thread
- ❧ template plastic
- ❧ black fineline permanent marker pen

Method

See the Templates on Pull Out Pattern Sheet 4 and the Quilt Diagram on page 169.

Preparation

1 For this quilt it is very important that your seam allowances are extremely accurate. To ensure this, make two seam marks on the plate of your sewing machine – one at 6 mm (^{1}/$_4$ in) and another one at 12 mm (^{1}/$_2$ in) for the arc seam adjustment.

2 With the coloured pencils, colour in the quilt diagram on page 7, according to your chosen fabrics, so you can use it for reference.

3 Arrange the fabrics in the order in which you have decided to use them.

For the arcs

4 Cut 5.5 cm (2^1/$_4$ in) wide strips of six fabrics for each colour grading. Strip-piece the strips into panels. Press all the seams in the same direction. Check the width of each fabric strip in the panel. Each one should be exactly 4.5 cm (1^3/$_4$ in) wide. If they are not, you have not kept a correct seam allowance and you will need to unpick and do it again.

5 Straighten one edge of the panel, then cut it into 6.4 cm (2^1/$_2$ in) wide strips. You will need twenty-four of each colour grading.

6 This step is extremely important: it holds the secret of success for this quilt. Having decided on your colour gradings, divide your two bundles of strips into halves so that one half has the lighter fabrics at one end and the other half has the reverse. Fold back the first fabric on the strip and resew the seam, starting at 6 mm (^{1}/$_4$ in) and increasing to that extra 6 mm (^{1}/$_4$ in) you have marked on the plate of your sewing machine (Fig. 1). Resew each seam for the arc in the same way. Place the arc on the ironing board and, with the inside curve of the arc facing you, press all the seams to the left. Before you go any further, check the curve of your arc with the arc template. If your curve is not as sharp as the template, pull the arc to fit and trim the ends. If your curve is too sharp and your arc is too short, you have increased your seams too much and will have to try again. If your arc fits well, sew all your other arcs in the same way.

Piecing

1 Using the templates, cut forty-eight melons and nine centres from the background fabric.

2 Set half of each arc group aside. Sew the other half to the melons in the following way. Mark the centre of the melon by finger-creasing it into quarters. Pin the centre to the centre seam of the arc (Fig. 2). Matching the ends of the arc to the edges of the melon, pin the edges together with the right sides facing. Stitch, pulling the fabric gently to shape it as you go (Fig. 3).

3 Cut the corner fabrics into squares for the four-patches, using the template. For this quilt you need sixteen of each of the four fabrics.

4 Stitch squares of one fabric to each end of half of the remaining melons, then attach the second colour to each end of the rest. Do the same for the other colour combination. Attach this lengthened arc to the arc-melon units, gently adjusting the shape as you go.

5 It is now time to lay out your quilt so all the pieces can be assembled, using your coloured quilt diagram as a guide. Finger-crease the centre piece along the centre line marked on the pattern. Pin the middle seam of the arc-melon unit to this line. Pin the ends of the centre piece to the arc-melon unit so that the end extends 6 mm (1/4 in) past the seam between the arc and the four-patch piece. Use a pin to mark the seam. Turn the seam towards the arc where possible. Stitch the units.

6 By alternating blocks, you will be able to assemble the rows of the quilt so that the edges are one continuous curved line (Fig. 4). First pin each row, then sew the entire seam. You will have three rows of three blocks.

7 Sew the rows together, then sew on the appropriate arc-melon units around the edge to complete the top. For the complete four-patch units around the edges and to avoid set-in corners, it is best to sew them to the arc-melon units before the arc-melon units are joined to the rows.

Quilting

Place the backing fabric face down with the wadding on top. Place the quilt top on top of that, face up. Baste the layers of the quilt together horizontally, vertically and diagonally. Quilt in the plain areas, either by hand or machine.

Binding

Because the quilt has curved edges, cut 7 cm (2³/4 in) wide bias strips for binding. Trim the wadding and the backing to the size and shape of the quilt top. Fold the binding over double, with the wrong sides facing. Sew the binding to the quilt, with the right sides facing and the raw edges even. Turn the folded edge of the binding to the back of the quilt and slipstitch it into place.

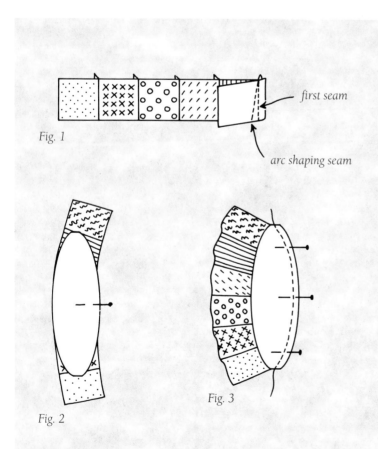

Fig. 1

first seam

arc shaping seam

Fig. 2

Fig. 3

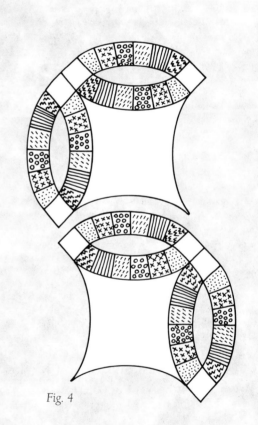

Fig. 4

Quilt Diagram

Baby's Silk Quilt

MADE BY PAT FLYNN KYSER

This feather-light silk quilt is a delight for a special baby. Embroider a garland of your favourite flowers in silk ribbons and a special motif in the centre, if you wish.

Materials

- ♣ 107 cm (42 in) square of silk batiste in the colour of your choice for the top
- ♣ 107 cm (42 in) square of white Swiss cotton batiste for the lining
- ♣ 107 cm (42 in) square of fine lightweight polyester wadding
- ♣ 107 cm (42 in) square of white Swiss cotton batiste for the backing
- ♣ 30 cm (12 in) strip cut across the width of the white Swiss batiste for binding
- ♣ 2 mm and 4 mm (^{1}/16 in and ^{3}/16 in) wide silk ribbons in your chosen colours for the flower embroidery
- ♣ DMC Stranded Cotton for embroidering the stems and leaves and the central motif
- ♣ Piecemaker tapestry needle
- ♣ Piecemaker embroidery needle, size 9
- ♣ Piecemaker quilting needle, size 9
- ♣ fine cotton quilting thread
- ♣ 66 cm (26 in) embroidery hoop
- ♣ water-soluble marker pen
- ♣ store-bought quilting templates for the corners

Method

Preparation

1 Fold the coloured silk batiste into halves, then into quarters, then into eighths and lightly finger-crease the folds to find the centre. Using the water-soluble pen, draw an arc across each eighth 30.5 cm (12 in) from the centre and again 15.25 cm (6 in) from the centre to form two scalloped circles 15.25 cm (6 in) apart.

2 Using the water-soluble pen and the embroidery hoop, mark a circle 66 cm (26 in) in diameter between the two scalloped circles. Baste in this circle. If you wish to embroider a motif in the centre, trace it with the water-soluble pen.

3 Fold the cotton batiste into halves, then into quarters and lightly mark the folds. Baste this piece to the back of the silk piece along the fold lines. Baste diagonally from corner to corner and around the edges. Baste around the circle on the silk batiste, catching the cotton batiste with each stitch. Working your embroidery through the two layers joined in this way will anchor the embroidery and prevent it from pulling through the delicate silk top.

Embroidery

1 Secure the centre of the piece in the embroidery hoop and embroider your central design with DMC Stranded Cotton. Make sure each stitch goes right through both pieces of fabric and ensure that thread ends are well hidden behind the cotton batiste.

2 Using the tapestry needle and your choice of silk ribbons, embroider a wreath of flowers, including wisteria, roses, rose buds, forget-me-nots and daisies, along the basted circle. Use the stitch guide on pages 184-187 to help you choose and work the flowers. Work randomly, going around the circle first with one kind of flower, then going back around the circle and filling in with another flower and so on. Do not make the flowers perfectly spaced or identical. You should try to create a spontaneous light and airy appearance.

3 Keep working around the wreath in this manner until it is as full as you want it to be. Go back and work in the stems and some leaves in both the DMC Stranded Cotton and silk ribbon. Again, try to avoid symmetry.

Quilting

1 Place the backing face down with the wadding on top and the embroidered top on top of that, face up. Baste through all the layers, horizontally, vertically, diagonally and around the edges.

2 Place the quilt top in the 66 cm (26 in) hoop. Using the quilting thread and quilting needle, quilt double lines 6 mm (¹/₄ in) apart, inside the inner scallop. Quilt a double diagonal grid from the embroidered centre to the inner scalloped circle. Place these grid lines 12 mm (¹/₂ in) apart. To create a true lattice-like appearance, weave these quilted lines over at one intersection and under at the next.

3 With single rows of stitches, firmly quilt the large scalloped ring outside the floral wreath.

4 Use a store-bought template, such as a feathered wreath or a heart, for the corner quilting patterns. Using the water-soluble pen, mark one in each corner.

5 Draw a 12 mm (¹/₂ in) diagonal grid from corner to corner of the quilt, ending at the outer scalloped circle and covering the areas not already quilted. Quilt along these lines, through all thicknesses. Quilt the designs in the corners as you come to them.

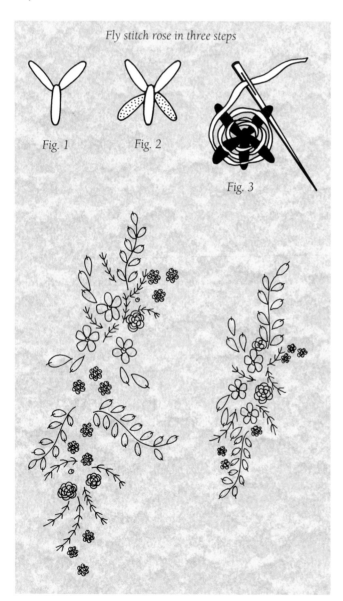

Fly stitch rose in three steps

Fig. 1   Fig. 2   Fig. 3

To complete

1 Cut the fabric for the binding into four 7.5 cm (3 in) strips. Fold them over double with the wrong sides together. Pin the binding to the sides of the quilt on the right side, with the raw edges matching. Stitch 12 mm (¹/₂ in) from the edge. Repeat for the top and bottom of the quilt. Turn the folded edge of the binding to the wrong side of the quilt and slipstitch it into place.

2 Embroider your name, the date, the baby's name and birth date on the back of the quilt.

3 Soak the quilt in clean cold water just long enough to remove all traces of the marker pen. Dry flat.

RIBBON ROSES

For as long as we can remember, red roses have signified passion and love. Even today, the gift of a dozen lovely red blooms clearly sends this unspoken message. White roses, on the other hand, signify purity – perhaps the reason they feature so prominently in bridal bouquets.

Lush full-blown roses are so evocative and feminine. Since you can't always be surrounded by the real thing, try making some of these lovely roses to have with you wherever you go.

Roses can be made in a number of ways – all quite simple. Three of these methods are described and illustrated in this section. Once you have mastered the very simple steps, you can make roses from fabric, ribbon, paper and lace, in any size you wish.

On page 176, there is a fabulous pink cabbage rose, made from ribbon, which you can use to trim a cushion or a pretty fabric-covered box.

Using a slightly different method and a variety of wondrous ribbons, you can make a whole bouquet of roses to trim a pair of shoes and matching purse, such as the one on page 178.

Finally, for the most romantic effect of all, see the Lace Roses on page 182. Here, beautiful Swiss lace has been formed into extravagant blooms which shine on a midnight-dark velvet background. Framed in an extravagant gold frame, the effect is truly fabulous.

Cabbage Rose Cushion

STITCHED BY GLORIA McKINNON

Lush cabbage roses are romantic and feminine and the perfect decoration for a cushion cover. For a natural look, make the rose from three shades of the one colour, from light to dark.

Materials

- ❦ 75 cm/30 in moire fabric
- ❦ 50 cm/20 in of 2.5 cm/1 in wide double-sided matte ribbon in a dark shade
- ❦ 1 m/40 in of 2.5 cm/1 in wide double-sided matte ribbon in a medium shade
- ❦ 2 m/2 yd of 2.5 cm/1 in wide double-sided matte ribbon in a light shade
- ❦ 50 cm/20 in of 2.5 cm/1 in wide double-sided matte ribbon in green
- ❦ sewing needle, sharp, size 8
- ❦ tapestry needle, size 20
- ❦ embroidery hoop
- ❦ sewing thread in the colour of the cushion
- ❦ green embroidery thread for the stems
- ❦ 30 cm/12 in cushion insert

Method

1 Cut two 28 cm/11¼ in squares for the cushion front and back. Cut three strips for the ruffle, 15 cm x 115 cm/ 6 in x 45 in.

2 Place the cushion cover front in the hoop and pull the fabric taut, then embroider the rose, buds and leaves.

Embroidery

To form the bud

Take a 10 cm/4 in length of ribbon and tie a loose knot in the centre then bring both tails of the knot together underneath the knot. Tease out the loops of the knot a little to adjust the shape of the bud. Cut the tails back to about 1.5 cm/¾ in. Stitch the bud to the cushion cover so that the tails lie flat and the bud stands upright.

To form the flower

1 Make a bud in the way described above. Cut four 9 cm/3½ in lengths of the medium shade of ribbon. Fold both ends of each piece down at an angle of 45 degrees. Run a curved line of basting along the lower edge of each length, catching the folded ends in the stitching. Pull up the basting to gather the ribbon, forming petals. Stitch each petal to the base of the bud in a natural-looking arrangement.

2 Make another group of petals in the light-coloured ribbon. You will need six or seven petals in the second row and eight or nine petals in the third row. In the last row, make only four or five petals going only halfway around the rose so that the centre doesn't look like a bullseye.

To form the leaves

Thread the tapestry needle with the green ribbon. Beginning on the wrong side of the cushion cover front, bring the needle up through the fabric close to the base of the rose. Lay the ribbon flat and take a stitch of the desired length (usually about 1 cm/½ in), reinserting the needle through the ribbon itself. This is called 'ribbon stitch' and it is this method which folds the ends of the leaves into a gentle point. When the leaves are in place, stitch lines of stem stitch in green embroidery thread to join the leaves and flowers together.

Assembling

1 Join the short ends of the ruffle strip to form a circle. Fold the strip over double with the wrong sides together. Divide the strip into quarters and mark the quarter points with a pin. Gather the raw edges together. Pin the ruffle around the cushion front, adjusting the gathering and matching the pin marks to the corners. Stitch the ruffle in place.

2 Place the cushion cover front and back together with the right sides facing and the ruffle in between. Stitch in the ruffle stitching line, leaving one side open. Turn the cushion cover to the right side. Place the insert inside the cover and slipstitch the opening closed.

Rose Shoes and Purse

MADE BY MARGARET B. WOLFE

This delightful set of evening shoes and matching bag is quite simple to make when you have mastered the basic rose.

All the roses are made in exactly the same way. The apparent variety is provided by the use of ribbons of different textures, widths and colours.

Materials

- ❧ **pump-style fabric-covered shoes**
- ❧ **purse, either purchased or handmade**
- ❧ **variety of ribbons including silk, velvet, metallic and French wired ribbon**
- ❧ **E6000 glue**
- ❧ **sewing needle**
- ❧ **sewing thread to match the ribbons**
- ❧ **chenille needle or tapestry needle**
- ❧ **hat pin or toothpick**
- ❧ **fine wire or Bouillion**
- ❧ **corrugated cardboard or styrofoam**
- ❧ **plastic wrap**
- ❧ **crinoline**

Method

For the rosebuds

1 For each rosebud, you will need seven times the width of the ribbon you are using. Beginning close to one end of the ribbon, fold down the end diagonally (Fig. 1).

2 Fold the width of the ribbon in half again, folding diagonally (Fig. 2). Fold again in the same manner (Fig. 3).

3 Insert a hat pin or a toothpick into the folds and roll the ribbon up around the pin or toothpick to form the centre of the rosebud (Fig. 4). Remove the pin, but keep a firm hold with your thumb and index finger to prevent it unrolling again.

4 Fold the loose part of the ribbon away from you, again folding on the diagonal. Still holding the base with your thumb and index finger, roll in the direction indicated by the arrow (Fig. 5). In order to roll the base of the rosebud along the inner edge of the ribbon, you will automatically force the

folded edge of the ribbon to remain at the top of the rosebud and flare out just slightly. When you have 'used up' the folded edge, fold the ribbon away from you again, just as you did the first time. Continue to fold and roll in this way until you have used all the ribbon, leaving a tail approximately 2.5 cm (1 in) long.

5 Sew a row of gathering stitches across the tail end of the ribbon (Fig. 6). Remove the needle but do not cut the thread. Draw up the gathering then secure the end to the base of the rosebud with a few stitches. Wrap the thread several times around the base of the rosebud, then secure it with a knot (Fig. 7).

For the full bloom

1 This rose is best worked with wired ribbon. You will need a length that is twelve to fourteen times the width of the ribbon. Every fold you make will stay in place if you crimp the wire slightly. Begin by following steps 1 to 5 for the rosebud to make a centre for the rose. Secure the base of the centre with a few stitches, then cut the thread.

2 Carefully remove the wire from the bottom edge of the remaining ribbon. Gather the bottom edge (Fig. 8). Loosely wrap the gathering around the base. Pinch in the loose end and secure it in place with some wire or with a few stitches.

3 Flatten the rose with your hand or, very gently, with a steam iron. Arrange the 'petals' attractively, crimping and pinching the wired edge to create a pleasing shape.

For the leaf

1 For this leaf, use a length of wired ribbon, seven to ten times the width of the ribbon. Carefully pull out 12 mm ($^1/_2$ in) of the wire from the same side of both cut ends of the ribbon. Gripping these ends of wire between your thumb and index finger, continue working the ribbon onto the wire until it is fully gathered (Fig. 9).

2 Pinch the cut ends together and wind the wire around to form the stem (Fig. 10).

3 To close the centre 'seam' of the leaf, apply a small amount of E6000 and press the edges together for a few seconds.

For the loop rosette

1 Use 30.5-35.5 cm (12-14 in) of 3 mm ($^1/_8$ in) metallic or silk ribbon. Using matching thread and a needle, take small stitches along the ribbon at approximately 2.5-4 cm (1-1$^1/_2$ in) intervals, beginning and ending approximately 2.5 cm (1 in) from the end of the ribbon (Fig. 11).

2 Pull up the thread to form the rosette. Secure the thread with a lock stitch (Fig. 12).

For the vines

Make shiny vines by coiling fine wire tightly onto a toothpick or chenille or tapestry needle. Remove the toothpick or needle, then pull the coil slightly to extend the vine. There is available a very tightly coiled super-fine wire material, called Bouillion, which is ideal. This delightful stuff comes in copper, silver and gold.

For the flat bud or leaf

1 Using a length of ribbon four times the width of the ribbon, fold one end down as shown in figure 13.

2 Cross-fold the ribbon and sew a gathering thread across (Fig. 14). Pull up the thread tightly, then wrap the thread around the ends of the ribbon to form a stem (Fig. 15).

Assembling

1 Cover a 25 cm (10 in) square of corrugated cardboard or styrofoam with plastic wrap. This will be your work surface.

2 Arrange your composition of roses, leaves, rosettes and vines on a piece of crinoline that is approximately the size of the shoe front or the purse flap. Remember to use black crinoline for dark colours and white for pastels. Any excess crinoline can be cut away from the back when the whole arrangement is assembled. Place the piece of crinoline on the work surface. Begin by placing the leaves and flat buds in position. Next, place your focal flower, usually the largest rose. Add in the smaller roses, rosebuds, leaves, loop rosettes and vines. These filler pieces can be tucked into empty spaces or be peeping out from behind a larger flower.

3 When you are pleased with your arrangement, glue it into place on the crinoline. Trim the crinoline from the back, then glue the crinoline into place on the shoes and the purse.

To learn know more about this charming craft, read *Small Treasures in Victorian Ribbonwork* by Margaret B. Wolfe.

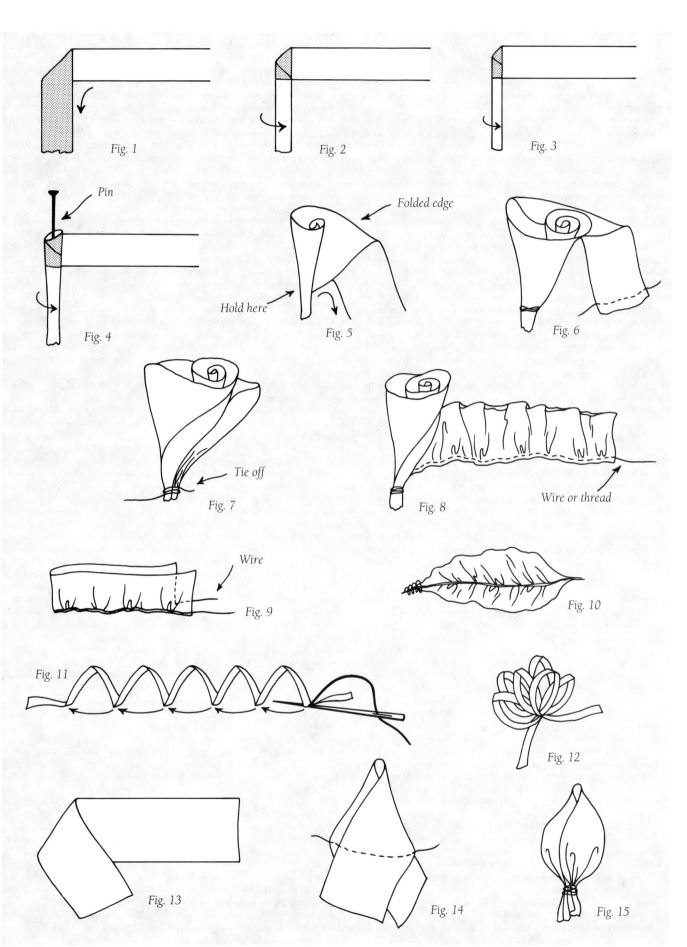

Fig. 1

Fig. 2

Fig. 3

Pin

Fig. 4

Folded edge

Hold here

Fig. 5

Fig. 6

Tie off

Fig. 7

Wire or thread

Fig. 8

Wire

Fig. 9

Fig. 10

Fig. 11

Fig. 12

Fig. 13

Fig. 14

Fig. 15

Lace Roses

MADE BY FAY KING

Ecru lace roses on a navy velvet background make this elegant piece that is really quite simple to create.

Materials

- ❦ 4.6 m (5 yd) of 10 cm (4 in) wide single-edge ecru Swiss needlerun lace
- ❦ 1.5 m (1²/₃ yd) of 12 mm (¹/₂ in) wide rayon ribbon, green
- ❦ 50 cm (20 in) of cotton velveteen, navy
- ❦ 50 cm (20 in) of Pellon
- ❦ one spool of cream quilting thread
- ❦ picture frame
- ❦ 1.5 m (1²/₃ yd) of 4 cm (1¹/₂ in) wide ribbon

Method

For the roses

1 Cut five pieces of lace, each 75 cm (30 in) long. Fold over the embroidered edge for approximately 2 cm (³/₄ in) at one end. Beginning at this end, roll the lace tightly four times for the centre of the rose. Using the quilting thread, stitch through the lace at the bottom to hold the centre securely.

2 Continue folding and rolling the lace around the centre, allowing the turns to become looser as you approach the outside of the rose. Stitch to secure as before.

3 Wrap quilting thread tightly around the base of the rose six or eight times, then trim any excess lace at the base. With your fingers, fold and arrange the top edge of the lace to resemble a rose.

For the buds

1 Cut three pieces of lace, each 25 cm (10 in) long. Roll the lace tightly for eight turns as for the centre of the rose, then fold the embroidered edge over and roll more loosely for the remainder of the length.

2 Stitch through the base with the quilting thread, then wind the thread around the base as before.

For the leaves

1 For each bud, cut two pieces of green ribbon, each 10 cm (4 in) long. Fold the ribbon as shown in figure 1.

2 Stitch across the base of the leaf, then pull up the stitching to gather the leaf. Stitch the leaves to the base of the buds.

Assembling

1 Baste the Pellon to the back of the velveteen. Arrange the five roses and three buds into a posy. Stitch each flower and bud securely to the velveteen, taking care that the velveteen does not pucker.

2 Tie a beautiful bow and attach it at the bottom of the posy with a few stitches.

3 Have your picture framed with a fabulous gilt frame which allows some depth.

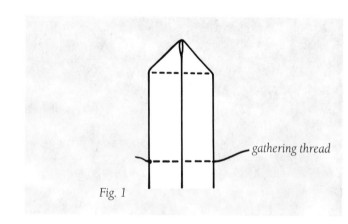

gathering thread

Fig. 1

Silk Ribbon Embroidery

Iris

Make these using 7 mm (⁷⁄₁₆ in) silk ribbon. Stitch the leaves and stems in straight stitches. Work an open fly stitch, then work a straight stitch through the securing loop at the bottom, allowing it to curve gently.

Wound Rose

Make these using 7 mm (⁷⁄₁₆ in) silk ribbon and matching thread.

Wind the ribbon loosely around a pin until you achieve the required size. Usually, three or four rounds will do.

With the matching thread make tiny stitches at intervals through the ribbon, allowing it to fall and fold gently. Make sure each loop is caught in the stitching. Remove the pin and secure the centre.

Back Stitch Rose

Working outwards from the centre, back stitch clockwise in a spiral, beginning with a stitch length of approximately 5 mm (¹⁄₄ in) for the first two rounds and lengthening to 1 cm (¹⁄₂ in) for the next two rounds.

Straight stitch

French knot   Work the centre of the rose in pistol stitch. Bring the ribbon through to the right side at the centre of the rose, then anchor a straight stitch at the required length with a French knot. You can vary the length of the centres.

Couched Rose

This rose is also worked in a spiral from the centre with the ribbon being couched at intervals with matching 4 mm (³⁄₁₆ in) silk ribbon. Continue making the spiral until you are pleased with the size and shape of your rose.

Fantasy Flower

The large blue flowers in the picture on page 77 are worked in large lazy daisy stitches and in straight stitches in contrasting 7 mm (⁷⁄₁₆ in) silk ribbon. Work a French knot in the centre.

The large pink flowers are worked in 7 mm (⁷⁄₁₆ in) ribbon stitch, left quite loose. the centre is a wool-padded ring with French knots inside.

Violet

Work the violet petals in straight stitches using 4 mm (³⁄₁₆ in) violet silk ribbon. Work a French knot in the centre using a gold thread.

Violet leaves are worked in blanket stitch, using 4 mm (³⁄₁₆ in) rich green silk ribbon.

Wheat

Using 4 mm (³⁄₁₆ in) yellow silk ribbon and beginning with a single straight stitch, continue working 'upwards' with open fly stitches.

Leaves

Groups of leaves are worked in the same way as the wheat, using 4 mm (³⁄₁₆ in) green ribbon. Small leaves are worked with straight stitches, using 4 mm (³⁄₁₆ in) silk ribbon.

Fuchsia

Fuchsias are made in 7 mm (⁷⁄₁₆ in) silk ribbon in two shades of pink.

For the base, using the paler pink and beginning with the bottom layer, work two straight stitches side by side with a third straight stitch worked loosely across the bottom of the first two.

Work a floppy open fly stitch at the top in the darker pink.

Form the stamens in pistol stitch (a straight stitch anchored at one end with a French knot) in the darker pink.

Primrose

Work a ring of blanket stitch in 4 mm (^{3}/$_{16}$ in) ribbon, leaving a centre of reasonable size. In the centre, work ribbon loops, anchored with French knots.

Ribbon Stitch

Bring the needle through from the back of the work at **a**. Take the needle through to the back by passing it through the ribbon at **b**. Don't pull the thread through too tightly or you will lose the little loop at the top.

Feather Flower

Work loops of 2 mm (^{1}/$_{16}$ in) silk ribbon in two rows with French knots in the centre of the rows.

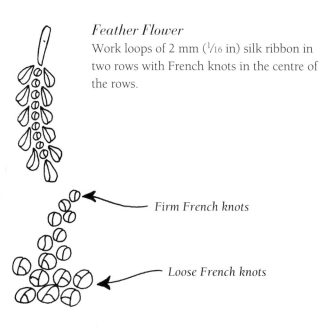

Firm French knots

Loose French knots

Lazy Daisy Stitch

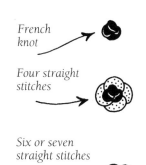

Lazy daisy stitch is the basic stitch for many embroidered flowers. Take care when you are working this stitch not to pull the ribbon too tightly or you will lose the softness of the ribbon.

For lazy daisy stitch, bring the needle through from the back at the centre point of the flower. Take the needle back through to the back of the work at a point very close to where it emerged.

Secure the loop you have just made with a tiny stitch across the loop, then bring the needle back to the centre ready to begin the next petal.

Grape Hyacinth

Using 2 mm (^{1}/$_{16}$ in) silk ribbon, work graded French knots from loose at the bottom to very tight at the top.

French Knot

French knots are ideal for flower centres. Begin by bringing the needle up through the fabric where you wish the knot to sit. Wind the ribbon around the needle twice. Gently pulling the thread tight, reinsert the needle near the point of exit and pull it through, bringing the needle out at the point you wish to make the next stitch.

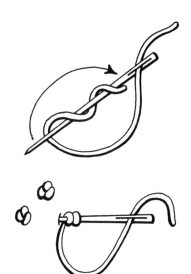

Silk rose

Tiny silk roses are worked in three shades of the same colour: a light, medium and dark.

Begin with a French knot centre in the darkest shade. Work four straight stitches around the centre in the medium shade, then work six or seven straight stitches around the outside in the lightest shade.

French knot

Four straight stitches

Six or seven straight stitches

For the rosebud, work a French knot in the centre in the darkest shade, then work two straight stitches on either side of the French knot in the medium shade.

Stem Stitch

Stem stitch is commonly used for outlines and, as the name implies, is mostly used for working the stems on flowers. Simply take a long stitch, bringing the needle out approximately half a stitch length back. Repeat this procedure along the required length, keeping the ribbon beneath the needle.

Tulip

Tulips are worked in ribbon stitch in various widths of silk ribbon.

Bring the needle through from the back of the work at **a**. Take the needle through to the back by passing it through the ribbon at **b**. Don't pull the thread through too tightly or you will lose the little loop at the top.

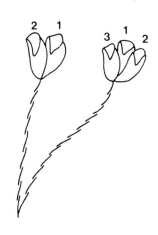

To form the tulip, use two or three ribbon stitches worked in the order indicated.

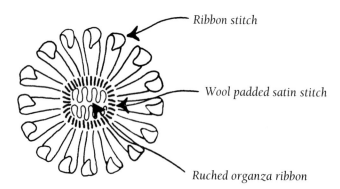

Ribbon stitch

Wool padded satin stitch

Ruched organza ribbon

Beige Flower

Work a ring of ribbon stitch in 7 mm (⁵⁄₁₆ in) wide ribbon, having the roll on the outer edge. The centre is a wool-padded ring with ruffled 7 mm (⁵⁄₁₆ in) organza ribbon.

Bullion Stitch

Bullion stitches are used either on their own, or in groups to create roses.

To make a bullion stitch, bring the needle through at **a** then take a stitch to **b**, bringing the needle back out at **a** without pulling the needle right through. Wrap the thread around the needle, covering the length from **a** to **b**. Pull the needle through and slide the wraps off the needle, easing them down until they are lying on the fabric. Reinsert the needle at **b** to secure the bullion.

Marigold or Gerbera

Stitch a ring of straight stitches in a matching colour wool. Stitch over this ring with straight stitches in silk ribbon.

Work two rounds of looped ribbon stitch around the padded ring. Work French knots in the centre.

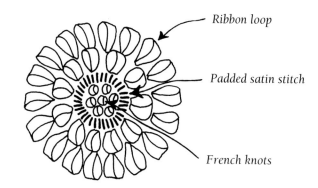

Ribbon loop

Padded satin stitch

French knots

Daffodil

Make these using 4 mm (³⁄₁₆ in) wide gold silk ribbon and working four lazy daisy stitches as for the daisy. To create the trumpet of the daffodil, work four buttonhole stitches as shown.

Crocus

This is another small flower which is made with lazy daisy stitch, just as it is worked for the daisy.

Place two lazy daisy stitches close together, even slightly overlapping. Work a bullion stitch centre.

Gloria's tips
for Successful Silk Ribbon Embroidery

I was first introduced to silk ribbon embroidery by Melva McCameron, an Australian living in the United States. It only took one day and I was hooked!

It is a very forgiving and rewarding form of embroidery. Forgiving because nature rarely forms a perfect flower so you don't need to either. If you make a flower you are not entirely happy with, just keep working until the picture is complete and then judge if you need to redo the flower. Most times, you will find you don't. It is rewarding because it covers so quickly that you will see results immediately.

Ribbons
As a general rule, I use Kanagawa silk ribbons in widths from 2 mm to 7 mm (¹⁄₁₆ in to ⁵⁄₁₆ in). Occasionally, I use a piece of rayon ribbon that has been overdyed.

I use a knot to begin, others don't; there are no right or wrong ways to do things – just different ways.

Work with short lengths of ribbon. This page is a good length to use. When you begin, thread the ribbon through the needle, then take the point of the needle back through the ribbon approximately 6 mm (¹⁄₄ in) from the end. This will allow you to use more of the ribbon (less waste) and save you searching around on the floor if the needle should fall.

Fabric
You can do silk ribbon embroidery on just about any fabric you can put a needle through. However, buy the best fabric you can afford. It takes just as long to embroider a cheap fabric as a good one but the results are very different.

If you are working on something that will need to be washed, take that into account when you are choosing your fabric.

Needles
I like to use Piecemaker tapestry needles in sizes from 20 to 26 (the higher the number, the smaller the needle).

Hoops
I always use a small hoop because I find it comfortable to do so and the work is even. Other people do lovely work without a hoop, so it is a matter of personal choice.

Stitches
Any stitch that can be successfully done with wool or thread can be done with ribbon. The only difference is that you do not pull the ribbon as tight as you do when working with thread.

Embroidery stitch books and stitch guides all have wonderful stitches just waiting to be stitched in ribbon. Ribbon also has the advantage of covering an area so much more quickly than threads can. Vintage linens are a great source when looking for design ideas. In my glory box days, it was called fancywork and the doilies, traycloths, tea cosies and tablecloths have an old world charm that we can reproduce for a nostalgia trip.

Designs
To transfer a design to your fabric, (I think linen looks best), photocopy the embroidered piece, then transfer to your fabric. This can be done in a variety of ways.

● Tape the photocopy up on a window or on a light box, then place the fabric over it and trace with a soft pencil.

● Using cheap tissue paper, trace the design from the photocopy with a transfer pencil. Lay the tissue paper with the pencilled side down and iron the design onto the fabric. This will be permanent, but it will be a mirror image.

● Place tulle or netting over the photocopy and trace the design using a biro or pen. Next, place the tulle or netting onto the fabric and, with a water-soluble pen or dixon pencil, draw over the lines. This will give you a series of dots which outline the design.

Flower books and gardening books are another source for embroidery designs, giving you colour and placement ideas. A group of French or colonial knots in purple colours, wider at the top and tapering to nothing will be wisteria – the same stitches wider at the bottom and tapering to nothing at the top will be hyacinths. Remember, you are only creating the illusion of a flower; you are not out to win a horticultural award!

Wool Embroidery

Wool Rose

Use two shades of pink, one light and one dark. With the darker pink, work four straight stitches beside one another. Still using the darker pink, work another four straight stitches over the top of the previous ones.

Using the lighter shade of pink and beginning three-quarters of the way along the side, work four straight stitches diagonally across one corner of the square. The fourth stitch is very small and is almost under the third one.

Continue in this manner, stitching over each corner of the square.

If the rose needs to be rounded out a little, moving clockwise, work small stem stitches around the outside.

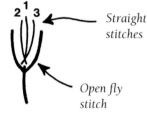

Straight stitches

Open fly stitch

Rose Buds

Using a darker pink, work three straight stitches, with the outer two crossing over slightly at the base. Work an open fly stitch in green around the outside of the bud.

Daisy

Daisy petals should always be worked from the centre outwards, following the order indicated.

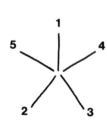

Stitch each petal, using lazy daisy stitch. When the petals are complete, work a French knot in the centre.

Rose Leaf

Begin with a straight stitch and then work as many open fly stitches as you need to give a nice leaf shape.

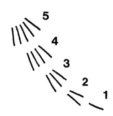

Lavender

Baste in a curved line as a guide. Using fine wool, work five straight stitches together, then four straight stitches, then three, then two, then one.

Forget-me-not

Use these small flowers as fillers. Make each petal as small as possible.

Using two strands of blue wool and following the steps for a five petal flower, work a tiny flower with straight stitches. Work three or four stitches into the same two holes for each petal. Work a French knot in the centre.

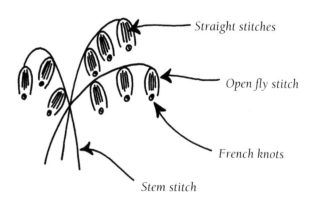

Straight stitches

Open fly stitch

French knots

Stem stitch

Lily of the Valley

Using two strands of fine white thread, work four straight stitches on top of one another. Work an open fly stitch in white so that the 'arms' extend beyond the centre stitches. Work a pale green French knot at the end of the centre stitches. Work the stems in stem stitch in pale green.

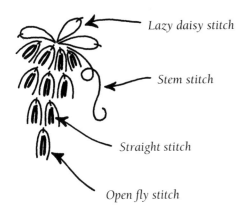

Lazy daisy stitch

Stem stitch

Straight stitch

Open fly stitch

Wisteria

Using a mushroom-coloured thick wool, work two stitches one on top of the other. Work open fly stitches around the flower centre in fine mauve wool.

Work large open leaves in green lazy daisy stitch and tendrils in green stem stitch.

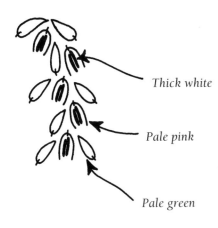

Thick white

Pale pink

Pale green

Wisteria Blossom

Using exactly the same stitches as for the wisteria, work the centres in thick white wool, the fly stitch in fine pale pink wool and the leaves and stems in pale green.

Iris

Work a lazy daisy stitch for the top of the flower, using two strands of fine wool. The outward leaning petals of the iris are indicated with a looped stitch through the back of the lazy daisy stitch. The loop can be worked in the same colour or in a mix of two different colours.

Work the stem with a single straight stitch in green and the leaves with long loose lazy daisy stitches.

Violet

Stitch the flower using a single purple thread. Make two large lazy daisy stitches at the top and three small ones at the bottom. Make a gold French knot in the centre.

For the bud, work a very small lazy daisy stitch in purple with a green open fly stitch around it. The stem is a long straight stitch. Work the leaves in green buttonhole stitch.

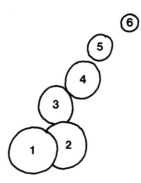

Filler Flower

This is a tiny flower that can be used as a filler, either in trails or bunches. Work two straight stitches on four sides of a small square with a French knot in the centre.

Hollyhock

The flowers are made up of wheels of buttonhole stitch, beginning with the largest one at the bottom and adding smaller ones up to the bud at the top. Make them curve slightly.

The leaves are also worked in buttonhole stitch but the stitch does not go into the same hole each time. Place the leaves along the base of the largest flower.

The buds are three buttonhole stitches with an open fly stitch surround.

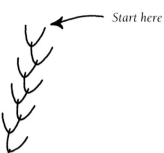

Start here

Fly Stitch Greenery
Work an interconnecting series of fly stitches, beginning at the top.

Buttonhole Stitch
Working from left to right, pull the needle through the fabric over the top of the working thread. Stitches can be worked side by side or spaced. To make a buttonhole stitch flower, simply work the stitches in a wheel as shown.

Feather Stitch
Very much like fly stitch, feather stitch is a pretty way to define a line. Begin at the top of the line and make alternate slanting stitches, pulling the needle through over the working thread.

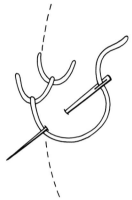

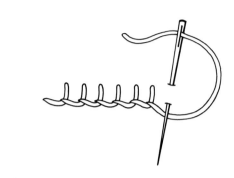

Gloria's tips
for Successful Wool Embroidery

Wool embroidery, like silk ribbon embroidery, is rewarding and forgiving. With a few tips, you can make one of the beautiful projects in this book.

Threads
Experiment with the variety of woollen threads available. In most cases, I have not specified which wool to use for a particular flower. Generally, you can choose one which suits you, the effect you wish to create, and is easily available. Some of the threads used in this book are: Appleton's Crewel Wool, Appleton's Tapestry Wool, DMC Tapestry Wool, DMC Medici Wool, Fancyworks Overdyed Wool, Royal Stitch Wool and Kacoonda Threads.

Always use a manageable length of thread. Generally, finger to elbow is the recommended length, but I have to confess, I leave it a little longer. I usually begin stitching with a knot.

Needles
You will need an assortment of needles in sizes from 18 to 24. I like to use Piecemaker tapestry needles, using the ones with larger eyes for tapestry wool and the ones with smaller eyes for crewel wool.

Fabrics
As a general rule, use the best quality fabric you can afford. The blankets in this book have been made using one hundred per cent pure Australian wool. This can be handwashed but I also wash blankets in my washing machine on a gentle cycle. Use a good quality wool wash and stay by the machine so you can stop the spin cycle before the blanket becomes felt. Spin only long enough to remove the excess water, then dry outside on the clothesline.

Transferring a Design
On the Pull Out Pattern Sheet, you will find some of the embroidery designs, given in detail. There are a number of methods for transferring an embroidery design to your fabric. Using transfer paper is probably the easiest. Simply trace the design from the pattern sheet, then transfer it using the transfer paper.

However, don't be too pedantic. This is a form of creative embroidery – so create! Use the pictures as a guide but don't worry if your flowers are in slightly different positions or are different colours. Embroider them in a way that pleases you.

Index

Angel 55

Angel bunnies 44

Appliqué, hand *see* Hand-appliquéd quilting

Appliqué cord 38

Baby's silk quilt 170

Baby's spring garden quilt 151

Back stitch rose 184

Baskets

    rose 100

    silk-lined 102

Bassinet blanket 18

Bear, teddy 125

Beige flower 186

Birdhouse, painted 60

Blankets

    in an English country garden 16

    bassinet 18

    cream-on-cream 10

    floral garden 12

    garden lambs 20

    rose 14

Boxes, découpage 130

    postcard 138

Brooches

    découpage 140

    embroidered with silk ribbon 80

Bullion stitch 37, 186

Bunnies, angel 44

Buttonhole stitch 120, 190

Cabbage rose cushion 176

Chatelaine, embroidered 48

Chevron stitch 120

Christening gown

    pillowcase 52

Christmas decorations

    angel 55

    wreath 98

Church dollies 32

Coathanger, velvet-covered 112

Couched rose 184

Crazy quilt 116

Crazy quilt purse 118

Cream-on-cream blanket 10

Cretan stitch 120

Crocus 186

Cushions

    see also Pillows

    cabbage rose 176

    silk ribbon embroidered 78

Daffodil 186

Daisy 188

Découpage 128

    box 130

    brooches 140

    postcard box 138

    screen 134

Dolls

    church 32

    dress 109

Double wedding ring quilt 166

Draught stopper 106

Dried flower wall picture 94

Embroidery 104-27

    see also sewing and embroidery

    see also Silk ribbon embroidery; Wool

embroidery

    chatelaine 48

    crazy quilt 116

    crazy quilt purse 118

    doll's dress 109

    draught stopper 106

    needle case 50

    pillow 121

    scissors case 50

    shadow 37

    smocking 109

    stitches 120

Fantasy flower 184

Feather flower 185

Feather stitch 120, 190

Filler flower 189

Floral flavours quilt 163

Floral foursome (dried flower picture) 94

Floral garden blanket 12

Flower basket picture 76

Flower crafts 92-103

    Christmas wreath 98

    floral foursome 94

    romantic swag 96

    rose basket 100

    silk-lined basket 102

Flowers, ribbon *see* Ribbon roses

Fly stitch greenery 190

Folk art 58-73

    birdhouse 60

    lamp 67

Forget-me-not 188

French knot 185

Fuchsia 184

Garden lambs blanket 20

Gerbera 186

Granitos 37

Grape hyacinth 185

Hand-appliquéd quilting

    hearts and hands wallhanging 158

    tips 162

Hand-quilting 157

Hearts and hands wallhanging 158

Heirloom sewing 30-57

    angel 55

    angel bunnies 44

    chatelaine 48

    christening gown pillowcase 52

    church dollies 32

    needle case 50

    nightgown 34

    peignoir 39

    scissor case 50

    stitches 37

    tips 43

Herringbone stitch 120

Hollyhock 189

In an English country garden blanket 16

Iris 184, 189

Lace roses 182

Lamp, painted 67

Lavender 188

Lazy daisy stitch 185

Leaves 184

Lily of the valley 188

Marigold 186

Monogrammed pillow 88

Needle case, embroidered 50

Nightgown 34

Nursery, paper tole 64

Painted birdhouse 60

Painted lamp 67

Pansy pillow 85

Paper tole 58-73

nursery 64

picture 70

Patchwork

crazy quilt 116

crazy quilt purse 118

Peignoir 39

Pictures

see also Paper tole;
Wallhangings

floral foursome (dried flowers) 94

flower basket (silk ribbon) 76

yesterday and today (silk ribbon) 82

Pillowcase, christening gown 52

Pillows

see also cushions

embroidered 121

monogrammed 88

pansy 85

silk ribbon embroidered 78

Postcards from the past quilt 154

Primrose 185

Purses

crazy quilt 118

ribbon rose 178

Quilting 142-72

hand- 157

hearts and hands wallhanging 158

patchwork purse 118

stipple 164

Quilts

baby's silk 170

baby's spring garden 151

crazy 116

double wedding ring 166

floral flavours 163

postcards from the past 154

seven sisters 144

twilight garden 148

Ribbon, silk embroidery see Silk ribbon embroidery

Ribbon roses 174-82

cabbage rose cushion 176

lace 182

rose shoes and purse 178

Ribbon stitch 185

Rondels 37

Rose basket 100

Rose blanket 14

Rose buds 188

Rose leaf 188

Rose shoes and purse 178

Roses, ribbon see Ribbon roses

Roses, sewn

back stitch 184

buds 188

couched 184

leaf 188

silk 185

wool 188

wound 184

Scissor case, embroidered 50

Screen, découpage 134

Seven sisters quilt 144

Sewing 104-27

see also Heirloom sewing; Quilting; Quilts

shoe stuffers 115

teddy bear 125

velvet-covered coathanger 112

Shaded eyelets 38

Shadow embroidery 37

Shawl, wool-embroidered 26

Shoe stuffers 115

Shoes, ribbon rose 178

Silk quilt, baby's 170

Silk ribbon embroidery 74-91

brooch 80

flower basket picture 76

monogrammed pillow 88

pansy pillow 85

pillows 78

stitches 184

tips 187

wallhanging 90

yesterday and today (picture) 82

Silk rose 185

Silk-lined basket 102

Smocking

doll's dress 109

tips 110

Split stitch 37

Spring blossoms 22

Stem stitch 186

Stipple quilting 164

Stitches

embroidery 120

heirloom sewing 37

silk ribbon embroidery 184

wool embroidery 28, 188

Swag, romantic 96

Teddy bear 125

Tulip 186

Twilight garden quilt 148

Velvet-covered coathanger 112

Violet 184, 189

Wallhanging

embroidered 90

hearts and hands 158

Wheat 184

Wisteria 189

Wool embroidery 8-29

bassinet blanket 18

cream-on-cream blanket 10

floral garden blanket 12

garden lambs blanket 20

in an English country garden blanket 16

rose blanket 14

shawl 26

spring blossoms 22

stitches 28, 188

tips 29, 190

Wool rose 188

Wound rose 184

Wreath, Christmas 98

Yesterday and today (picture) 82